Why Evil?

The Solution to God's Creation Dilemma—Why Evil Had To Be Part of God's Creation

Michael K. Pasque

For since the creation of the world God's invisible qualities—his eternal power and divine nature—have been clearly seen, being understood from what has been made, so that men are without excuse.

Romans 1:20 (all scriptural passages from NIV)

PREFACE

All of us who have spent time studying the text of the Bible have encountered "inconsistencies" that don't seem to mesh well with our theology. Sometimes it isn't just a matter of "meshing well"—these inconsistencies can be downright opposed to our theology!

This theology of ours is obviously important to us. It forms our perspective regarding how God relates to our life. As such, our personal theology is vital and it is mandatory. God demands a theology of every human being. We all, no matter what we profess to believe, must answer the question of God's relationship to our existence.

It is our response to this question that frames the perspective, the lens with which we view the events of our life. This is important because it is precisely our perspective that determines how we respond to these events. Perspective determines behavioral response, good or bad. It is therefore critical to our life decisions that we develop an accurate theology. In regard to "accuracy," the only applicable metric is Holy Scripture. Our goal, therefore, must be a theology, a perspective that agrees with the text of Holy Scripture.

In the process of developing an accurate theology, we can expect to encounter resistance. Most of this resistance will come from within. Because of the obvious importance that our theology holds in our life, we naturally want to defend and preserve it. After all, for most of us it represents the culmination of many years of encountering our unique and personal set of life events.

So, as distressing as these scriptural inconsistencies may be, in the vital preservation of our personal theology we usually choose to summarily dismiss them as being those "mysteries" that cannot be understood by mere mortals. We assume that God understands these difficult Biblical passages—and that is enough. We dismiss them as mysteries whose presence we dutifully accept as a matter of faith. This dismissal allows us the best of both worlds: we can continue to grasp firmly to our personal theology by a pious act of faith! We have faith that God understands these issues and can explain how they fit quite nicely into—*and agree with*—the very comfortable theology that we have adopted as reality. When confronted, we somewhat irreverently respond, "We'll just have to wait and have Jesus explain that one to us."

As comforting as it may be, our "humble act of faith" is entirely misguided. Instead, our charge must be to confront the inconsistencies that exist between our theology and the written word of God. This, by definition, must be a long process—a lifelong adventure. In this Spirit-driven process, our theology must continue to morph as God reveals more of Himself to us.

So, in regard to these "inconsistencies," we *must* assume that the problem is not an "inconsistency" in the Bible, but an error in our theology. It is our theology that needs reworking, not the scriptural passages in question. Instead of "cherry-picking" the parts of the Bible that agree with our theology, we should instead—as if on a challenging adventure—seek to modify our cherished theology, moving it toward agreement with *every* passage of Holy Scripture.

That which stands in our way is that which must be purged in the process of our sanctification. Preservation of *self* drives all and muddies the process. Our self tells us that we have it right.

Self never wants to change. In fact, it is incapable of voluntarily changing. It wants us to mold our understanding of Holy Scripture to fit the theology that allows it to tend comfortably with the self-centered perspective that generates our selfish ways.

Abandonment of self is the only solution. It alone solves the theology issue. Our inability to give up that to which we cling in order to preserve that which self desires, alone stands as an opacity between the eyes of our heart and that which we must see.

As a result of our inability to abandon self to God, so many of us spend our lives dancing around the edges of the consuming fire, the illuminating light, the eternal truths that emanate from the Uncreated God—never allowing ourselves the full engagement found in total immersion. We feel the warmth of consuming fire, live life illuminated by light reflected from infinitely pure holiness, and remain only intermittently sated in our desire for eternal truth.

All the while we are restrained—self-restrained—never allowing ourselves anything more than to venture near the edge of the fiery realm. Deep in our anxious hearts, we want to leap into it rather than dallying near its edge. We know it is precisely that for which we were created. We know it is our destiny.

And yet our humanity, our sinful nature, our preservation of self, and our fear keep us only partially sated in the lukewarm bath of what we believe to be safety at its edges—a mere step away from the fierce selflessness, the consuming fire of that for which we were created. The dross of our fear remains unconsumed by the Uncreated Fire through which we must pass. We hesitate—sometimes for the entirety of our life—teetering precipitously and fearfully into that which is nothing less than the deepest desire of our infinitely deep hearts and the eternal

Fellowship for which we were made. For most of us, a leap into the Uncreated Fire is long over due.

Chapter One

NANOSECONDS BEFORE THE BIG BANG

Scientists around the world are spending billions of dollars trying to recreate the early nanoseconds following the event referred to as the "Big Bang." Their motivation finds its foundation in the proven track record of such efforts to describe and decipher the electromagnetic data emanating from the early moments of the universe. As the clock has been wound backward into the nearly immeasurable time fragments immediately following that moment when the universe came into existence, much has been uncovered regarding its origins.

And yet these efforts leave many of us puzzled in regard to the real impact of the knowledge thereby revealed. Although the answers to these questions no doubt hold great import to the astrophysicists of the world, most of us common earth dwellers expect very little trickle-down impact on our day-to-day existence.

In stark contrast, a close examination of what God has revealed regarding the micro-fragmented time on the *other side* of the Big Bang holds the potential to fill the seeking heart with knowledge of potentially profound impact. In these moments are found the answers to the many "Why?" questions that fill our curious and troubled minds regarding the makeup of the creation—why certain things were included and others not.

Our quest, therefore, is exposure of a tiny fragment of the thoughts of God occurring nanoseconds *prior* to the Big Bang.

In this regard, God reveals much in the written word of His prophets. Not surprisingly, this scriptural evidence speaks of *our* place in God's creation. Indeed, an examination of the scriptural evidence suggests that it was almost exclusively upon us that God's thoughts were centered in those timeless moments preceding the creation. Further, the evidence suggests that our *raison d'etre* was at the very heart of a dilemma faced by God moments before He lit the fuse of His creation masterpiece.

We take obvious liberties in labeling this a "dilemma" for God, since, as the Creator God, His intellect is of course absolute in every respect. It is, nonetheless, precisely this *dilemma* that we seek to explore. Moreover, we also take considerable liberty in referencing God's thoughts to a particular increment of time. We do, of course, use any such time references as a *construct*, fully recognizing that God and the topic of His thoughts prior to the creation exist without limits— entirely outside of the limiting constraints of even the smallest increment of time.

When the word "dilemma" is referenced to God in Christian discourse, it often prompts discussions regarding the presence of evil in the creation. In this regard, the focus is usually on such topics as the evil defined by man's inhumanity to man, horrible things happening to good people, or the truly hopeless plight of fallen mankind. As we will discuss, however, God's real dilemma was not centered on the presence of evil—evil in fact being a critical part of the *solution* to His true dilemma. We will begin at the beginning.

Chapter Two

OUR CREATION PURPOSE

Там here was no beginning. The Fellowship has always existed—the Father, the Son, and the Holy Spirit always swirling in the subservience-motivated movement of the infinite dance of truly loving fellowship that *is* the eternal kingdom of God. We are told, *"God is love"* (1John 4:16). From this revelation, we can know much about this Fellowship. First and foremost, we can know that God's deepest heart desire is to love, *not* to *be* loved.

> *Whoever does not love does not **know** God, because God is love. This is how God showed his love among us: He sent his one and only Son into the world that we might live through him. This is love: not that we loved God, **but that he loved us** and sent his Son as an atoning sacrifice for our sins. Dear friends, since God so loved us, we also ought to love one another. (1John 4:8-11; emphasis added)*

> *We love because he first loved us. (1John 4:19)*

We can therefore be assured that the creation—our creation—had no other motivating source than the deep heart love of God. We came into existence as a result of the spontaneous, uninhibited, and unrelenting desire of God to *share* the loving Fellowship of the Trinity. Sharing, after all, must be the natural product of the infinitely deep subservient sacrificial love that is the foundation of this Fellowship. We sprang forth, therefore, not in response to a *need*, but rather as the only possible consequence of the ferocious love of the Trinity that is forever manifest in their eternal Fellowship.

Ferocious. What a word. But, to share in that Fellowship, to so infinitely and subserviently love each Member of the Fellowship, to be so devoid of "self" as to seek nothing else except the desires of its Members—this is the love of the Fellowship of God and it cannot be anything less than ferocious. In fact, so ferocious is this love that "sharing" is its natural product, its inexorable, uncompromising, unstoppable, and uncontainable consequence. *Sharing* is *of* that Fellowship like the searing bright white flash *of* a nuclear explosion. It is unrelenting. It permeates all and illuminates all and cannot be restrained. *Sharing* is an inseparable part of the love of the Fellowship.

> *The life appeared; we have seen it and testify to it, and we proclaim to you the **eternal life**, which was with the Father and has appeared to us. We proclaim to you what we have seen and heard, **so that you also may have fellowship with us**. And **our fellowship** is **with** the Father and with his Son, Jesus Christ. We write this **to make our joy complete**. (1John 1:2-4; emphasis added)*

God simply could not help Himself, so unyielding is his desire to infinitely and perfectly love by sharing the Fellowship. And so, God moved to create beings to love, beings to share in the indescribable glory *and love* of the eternal Fellowship of the three Persons of the Triune Godhead.

> *His divine power has given us **everything we need for life and godliness through our knowledge of him who called us** by his own glory and goodness. Through these he has given us his very great and precious promises, so that through them **you may participate in the divine nature** and escape the corruption in the world caused by evil desires. (2Peter 1:3-4; emphasis added)*

The creation was therefore a direct consequence of God's love. Its purpose is to produce, foreknow, call, justify, and glorify beings to inhabit the eternal kingdom of God as royal heirs: princes and princesses to share in the bright-light Fellowship of the Trinity forever.

> *For those God foreknew he also predestined to be conformed to the likeness of his Son, that he might be the firstborn among many brothers. And those he predestined, he also called; those he called, he also justified; those he justified, he also glorified. (Romans 8:29-30)*

Chapter Three

PERFECT AND SOVEREIGN

Thus, just nanoseconds before that Big Bang signaled the onset of this most preposterous demonstration of the truly selfless love of our Creator, He faced a dilemma. Two facts serve as a prequel to—and help frame—this "dilemma." The revelation of both is readily apparent not only in the world around us, but also in the written word of God.

First, as Tozer—referencing the entourage of ancient saints from whom he drew the breath of the Spirit—has so eloquently defined in The Knowledge of the Holy, God is *perfect*. Infinitely perfect. In everything that He is and everything that He does, God is perfect. This we can know beyond any shadow of a doubt. Logically speaking, this makes sense. After all, who else defines "perfect" as an adjective describing anything in the creation except the Creator God Himself?

The second fact that helps frame God's dilemma is the glorious truth of His sovereignty. God is *sovereign* over everything. There is nothing in His creation over which He does not rule with perfect authority. In this regard, God is all-powerful, omnipotent. No one can exert his or her will over God's will.

The combination of these two facts reveals that God's perfection rules the creation. God is perfect and since He is sovereignly omnipotent over His creation, so also is His creation. God, as Sovereign Creator, defines and enforces His perfection in the creation as an obligatory fact. This is not negotiable. In His creation, things *are* exactly as God wants them to be. He makes certain of that.

> The LORD said to me, *"You have seen correctly, for I am watching to see that my word is fulfilled."* (Jeremiah 1:12)

And yet every breathing human being knows something—by experience if not by the written word of God—that doesn't just conflict with that statement, but seems to fly violently in the face of all who would describe God's creation work as "perfect." That *something* is known as "evil." Evil doesn't just exist in God's creation; it is in fact pervasive throughout His creation. How can the word "perfect" be applied to a creation in which the ravages of evil are expansive and so readily apparent to even the most disinterested?

This fact of God's mandatory perfection in all of His work has much to reveal regarding the machinations of evil played out since the beginning of recorded history. The fact of God's perfection assures us that everything that is going on around us is not just *allowed* by God, but also indeed *sent* by God. God's inherent perfection assures us that not only is all that occurs in this creation precisely the plan of our Sovereign Creator God, but that in regard to His will—His sovereign eternal will—it is also perfect. Every part of the creation—including the playing out of evil's game in all of our lives—is in fact God's perfect will.

In other words, God's creation purpose—to create and sanctify those sons and daughters of God who were predestined before time to spend eternity in loving fellowship with the three Persons of the Trinity and with each other—must be, by definition, only and most perfectly attained by that which we see around us. The creation had a purpose, and we are that purpose.

*For while we are in this tent, we groan and are burdened, because we do not wish to be unclothed but to be clothed with our heavenly dwelling, so that what is mortal may be swallowed up by life. Now it is God who has **made us for this very purpose** and has given us the Spirit as a deposit, guaranteeing what is to come. (2Corinthians 5:4-5; emphasis added)*

So, no matter how corrupted, nefarious, and downright evil this world may appear to us right now, it is perfect in regard to the attainment of its creation purpose. It is precisely as God so thoughtfully—with fathomless wisdom—and so infinitely perfectly planned it to be. It must be perfect—even right this minute in the midst of the preposterous mess we see around us—if the creation, as a whole, is to be taken as perfect—which it must. Indeed, this disheartening mess that we see around us *must* be perfect to achieve that for which it was originally brought into being. This fact is that which empowers us to very literally praise God and express thanksgiving in every situation, no matter how bad. Even in the midst of the biggest disasters, we can praise Him and thank Him because we know that what we are going through is—in the context of God's sovereignty and His love for us—perfect.

Be joyful always; pray continually; give thanks in all circumstances, for this is God's will for you in Christ Jesus. (1Thessalonians 5:16-18)

We can be assured that two hundred thousand years from now God will not be sitting on His throne lamenting over not having done things differently. He will, as Sovereign Creator, *have* precisely the eternity that He desires. The end product of all of His creation effort—from its beginning to its end—will be perfect. It cannot be any other way. God is simply, by His very nature, incapable of spending eternity with anything less than absolute perfection. Imperfection, especially in fellowship, is not just a casual annoyance to God. It is intolerable. It will not happen.

The conclusion is clear. As part of that creation purpose solution, all that we see around us, including the evil, the rebellion, the darkness of man's heart—and the sin that results—is therefore guaranteed to be part of the perfect solution to God's perfect creation purpose. Further, you and I, the product of this creation, will be—in Christ—made perfect by precisely this creation for an eternity of *life* in the loving Fellowship of the Triune Godhead.

> *But when this priest had offered for all time one sacrifice for sins, he sat down at the right hand of God. Since that time he waits for his enemies to be made his footstool, because by one sacrifice* **he has made perfect forever those who are being made holy**. *(Hebrews 10:12-14; emphasis added)*

So, if evil is in fact a perfect part of the perfect creation process by which God perfectly achieves His perfect creation purpose, then what exactly is going on here? What is this all about? Why was evil—and all of the immeasurable human suffering that results from evil—so necessary to God's master plan?

The answer is found in the revelation of the solution to God's dilemma.

Chapter Four

GOD'S DILEMMA

To understand God's dilemma, we must first understand ourselves. We must understand our deep heart. We must grasp the amazing attributes of the deep heart connection that we share with God. This connection has, of course, come about by the precise design of our Creator God. Inherent to our heart is our creation purpose. As discussed, we were created to join the eternal Fellowship of God as His sons and daughters.

> *"I will be a Father to you, and you will be my sons and daughters, says the Lord Almighty."* *(2Corinthians 6:18)*

Also inherent to our heart is its deepest indwelling *desire*. Our creation purpose and our deepest heart desire are obviously directly interrelated and form the foundation of the deep heart connection that we share with our Creator.

Further, both our creation purpose and our God-ordained deepest heart desire find their center in God's ultimate goal: our eternity in the subservient, sacrificial loving Fellowship of the Trinity.

> *"Father, I want those you have given me **to be with me where I am**, and to see my glory, the glory*

*you have given me because you loved me **before** the creation of the world. (John 17:24; emphasis added)*

We were made for this Fellowship. When we join this Fellowship, it will represent the full achievement and fulfillment of our creation purpose.

*For you know that we dealt with each of you as a father deals with his own children, encouraging, comforting and urging you to live lives worthy of God, **who calls you into his kingdom and glory.** (1Thessalonians 2:11-12; emphasis added)*

*His intent was that now, through the church, the manifold wisdom of God should be made known to the rulers and authorities in the heavenly realms, according to **his eternal purpose** which he accomplished in Christ Jesus our Lord. In him and through faith in him **we may approach God with freedom and confidence.** Ephesians 3:10-12; emphasis added)*

Our God-ordained deepest heart desire, therefore, is most certainly not to *be loved*, as so many profess. Instead, our deep heart desire is to subserviently and sacrificially love God (and each other). For in order for us to be perfect for the Fellowship, God made us in His image—He made our deepest heart desire just like *His* deepest heart desire. The three Persons of the Triune Godhead have as their deepest heart desire the subservient, sacrificial love of each other. So also then, since our creation purpose is to join the eternal loving Fellowship of God, God made our deepest heart desire the same as those with

Whom we will enjoin in fellowship: to subserviently and sacrificially love everyone in the Fellowship.

And, precisely herein lies God's dilemma—for to love someone, you must *know* them. In fact, the more you know someone, the more capacity you have to love them—and the deeper and more profound is the resulting loving fellowship. Deep, for instance, is the love found between the elderly husband and wife who have spent a lifetime deeply engaged in and running hard after the knowledge of each other.

This may not seem obvious at first glance, but God's dilemma was how to go about doing nothing less than the impossible. He had to come up with a way to teach the created all about the *Uncreated*. He had to impart to us knowledge of Himself. As pointed out above and restated here below, this is precisely what the Christian life is all about—the gaining of knowledge of God so that we can join the eternal Fellowship in love.

> *His divine power has given us **everything we need for life and godliness through our knowledge of him who called us** by his own glory and goodness. Through these he has given us his very great and precious promises, so that through them **you may participate in the divine nature** and escape the corruption in the world caused by evil desires. (2Peter 1:3-4; emphasis added)*

Our participation *"in the divine nature"* described in this Scriptural passage is indeed nothing less than our entering into the Fellowship of the Trinity.

God's dilemma is a bigger problem than we might initially think. Why? To solve this problem, God in fact had to bridge an unbridgeable gap. Giving us knowledge of the *Uncreated* that would allow our eternal fellowship in that great Presence, that Uncreated Presence, that Eternal Divine Fellowship, is a task, a dilemma, a conundrum of such magnitude that it is simply incomprehensible to us, the created.

After all, what can the created really know about the *Uncreated*? What can we know about a Being *"who alone is immortal and who lives in unapproachable light, whom no one has seen or can see" (1Timothy 6:16)*? When challenged by the conundrum of "the *Uncreated*," the honest man can only respond as did Jeremiah:

> *No one is like you, O LORD; you are great, and your name is mighty in power. Who should not revere you, O King of the nations? This is your due. Among all the wise men of the nations and in all their kingdoms, there is **no one like you**. (Jeremiah 10:6-7; emphasis added)*

By definition, everything that we, the created, can "know" must be *created*—it must exist in the creation around us and be perceivable in that creation by the creation participants. Thus, even what we know about the Uncreated God, by definition, must be created—it must be a *construct* in the creation that conveys knowledge of God. Surely this created construct of the Uncreated God can only be best described as *"a poor reflection as in a mirror."*

> *Now we see but a poor reflection as in a mirror; then we shall see face to face. Now I know in part; then I shall know fully, even as I am fully known. (1 Corinthians 13:12)*

Further, God couldn't just provide to His created beings a simple didactic lecture-given knowledge of Himself—knowledge that would be adequate only for a limited and relatively superficial loving relationship. Instead, if these created partners were to be fully functional participants in the eternal Fellowship of the Uncreated Trinity, God knew he had to provide them with truly *deep* heart knowledge of Himself.

Thus, in those infinitely brief non-time moments immediately prior to the dawn of creation, God crafted and set into motion the perfect plan to solve His dilemma—to give us that knowledge of Him that we must have in order to join Him for eternity. His plan was nothing short of spectacular. His plan was for the members of the body of Christ to *"reach unity in the faith and in the **knowledge** of the Son of God and become mature, attaining to the whole measure of **the fullness of Christ**"* (Ephesians 4:13; emphasis added).

God took on the task of giving us a *"fullness,"* a knowledge of Him that would allow nothing less than the deep loving Fellowship enjoyed for all eternity by the Members of the Trinity. To *"become mature"* is indeed to attain the knowledge of God that enables us to love as amazingly as They love. This can happen only if we are in Christ. This can happen only if we have put off our *"old self with its practices and have put on the new self, which is being renewed in **knowledge** in **the image of its Creator**"* (Colossians 3:9-10; emphasis added). It is remarkable how many times Scriptural passages refer to, and emphasize the all-encompassing importance of the *knowledge of God*.

Remarkably, understanding God's solution to this dilemma is precisely the necessary roadmap to gaining the answers to our questions regarding the presence of evil in the creation—and why God puts us through that which we experience in this life, with all of its adventures, trials, and tribulations.

In him we were also chosen, having been predestined according to the plan of him who works out everything in conformity with the purpose of his will, (Ephesians 1:11)

In this knowledge that we were chosen by God, we find hope. Our future is guaranteed. Nonetheless, our knowledge of God is currently incomplete. It is inadequate to enable the love of God and each other that is required of the eternal Fellowship of God. We are immature. We know only *"in part."* But our hope is sure because it is placed in a faithful God who has promised that our knowledge of Him will be complete. One day, we will know Him *"fully."*

*For we know **in part** and we prophesy **in part**, but when perfection comes, the imperfect disappears. When I was a child, I talked like a child, I thought like a child, I reasoned like a child. When I became a man, I put childish ways behind me. Now we see but a poor reflection as in a mirror; **then we shall see face to face**. Now I know in part; then I shall know **fully**, even as I am fully known. (1 Corinthians 13:9-12; emphasis added)*

Chapter Five

GOD'S SOLUTION TO HIS DILEMMA: PART I

S o, God's dilemma was straightforward. Subservient, sacrificial love is the foundation of the loving Fellowship shared for eternity by the three Persons of the Triune Godhead. It is for this Fellowship that we have been created. It is to this Fellowship that we have been invited. As we have discussed, by nothing less than God's precise design, entrance into this Fellowship is not only our creation purpose, but also our God-ordained deepest heart desire.

To be made capable of loving the three Persons of the Trinity (and our fellow saints) in a subservient and sacrificial fashion is the one and only *capability* that is prerequisite to joining this Fellowship and thereby to achieving our creation purpose and sating our deepest heart desire. How best to perfectly and infinitely endow created beings with this God-given capability to love was the dilemma faced by our Creator God in the nanoseconds preceding the Big Bang.

God's solution to this dilemma is important. It impacts every one of us and is pervasive through every moment of every day of our life. This solution was found in meeting two readily defined requirements. Not only must the created beings 1) be taught *how* to truly love in a subservient, sacrificial manner, but they must also 2) be enabled with a *knowledge* of the objects of that love—the three Persons of the Triune Godhead (and our fellow saints)—that allows a love that is *worthy* of the magnificent Fellowship to which they had been invited.

The first requirement is the topic of this chapter. Teaching us *how* to truly love, is achieved by nothing less than making us the object of the greatest single manifestation of subservient, sacrificial love in all eternity—the incarnation, crucifixion death, and resurrection of Jesus Christ. In this, Jesus becomes our perfect role model. His life, death, and resurrection become the example for us to emulate. In this example is offered the *only* avenue for learning *how* to love God.

> *This is how we know what love is: Jesus Christ laid down his life for us. And we ought to lay down our lives for our brothers. (1John 3:16)*

Further, God enhances this example even further by mandating on-the-job training in each of our lives. He makes this very personal by making the mandatory requirement for salvation nothing less than the casting off of our self-life. We die to "self"—which is the very definition of subservient, sacrificial love—in our acknowledgment of the subservient nature of the truly sacrificial love displayed by Jesus on the cross. Only in bowing our hearts and fully surrendering to the love of Jesus are we saved and thereby join the Fellowship to which He has destined us.

Amazingly, we are then mercifully allowed to subserviently and sacrificially mimic (in our miniscule way) God's extraordinary love. In doing this, we learn subservience and sacrificial love by Christ's example. We learn by doing. When *"we love one another, God lives in us and his love is made complete in us"* (1John 4:12). We love Jesus and acknowledge His example by subserviently and sacrificially loving one another in His Name. This places the cross of Christ front and center in our life every day. In our mirroring acts of love, we acknowledge the completeness of the work of Christ and are thereby enabled in our work of loving one another only by the power of the cross of Christ.

In other words, we learn how to love subserviently and sacrificially not just by being the object of Jesus' most extraordinary example, but also by observing and emulating His perfect example. This takes a lifetime. Indeed, our sinful nature creates in us thoughts, desires, and actions that can only be described as the darkest of evil. Our selfish treatment of our fellow human beings places us not in fellowship with the three Persons of the Trinity, but instead at the polar opposite of that eternal Fellowship. We have not only witnessed and cheered the manifestations of evil in our lives, we have become that evil. Our outright dark rebellion against the bright white holiness of our sovereign loving Creator so far separates us from the unknowable purity of the Uncreated Triune Godhead that the gulf itself can only be described by the most laborious use of the word *infinite*.

> *But your iniquities have separated you from your God; your sins have hidden his face from you, so that he will not hear. (Isaiah 59:2)*

Nonetheless, even in our most despicable state, we are offered the most merciful of solutions to an unsolvable predicament. In recognition of all that has been done for us, our ultimate act of subservient, sacrificial love in this life is the same for every one of us. Each of us must cast off all care for "self" in that moment in which we give all to Jesus Christ in our recognition of the salvation work that was selflessly done for us on the cross of Calvary. His shed blood is our only solution.

In humbly and subserviently accepting this gift of atonement for our sins, we volitionally place ourselves below our Savior. We place His will, His desires, and His commands above our own. In this "dying to self" we also learn to put the desires of all—including not only the Trinity, but also our fellow saints—above our own.

> *Do nothing out of selfish ambition or vain conceit, but in humility consider others better than yourselves. Each of you should look not only to your own interests, but also to the interests of others. (Philippians 2:3-4)*

Truly the circumstances of this moment of our salvation are unique to each one of us, but to all of us this moment represents the pinnacle of subservient sacrificial love in our life. So also was the crucifixion of our role model, Jesus Christ, the pinnacle of all subservient sacrificial love for all eternity. And thus it is our God-ordained very great privilege to mimic the love of Jesus as we step into the eternal Fellowship of the King.

Understanding that this foundation of subservient, sacrificial love defines the nature of our relationship to Jesus is critical. After all, if subservient, sacrificial love is the foundation of the eternal Fellowship of the three Persons of the Trinity, then it is *everything*. It is unsurpassed in importance when compared to anything else that we shall carry from this life into the next.

The ability to love in such a manner cannot be conveyed in even the most complex of didactic lectures. Indeed, a capability of such profound importance can only be learned by observation of—*and by participation in*—the passion of Christ. To learn it to the infinitely perfect degree—an obligatory step if we are to enjoy an eternity of loving fellowship with *the Uncreated*—not only must we observe, but so also become the desperate and hopelessly lost object of that perfectly modeled love…and then reciprocate in loving one another. In this daily reciprocation is both the "working out" of our salvation—

*Therefore, my dear friends, as you have always obeyed—not only in my presence, but now much more in my absence—continue to **work out your salvation** with fear and trembling, for it is God who works in you to will and to act according to his good purpose. (Philippians 2:12-13; emphasis added)*

—and the filling up in our *"flesh what is still lacking in regard to Christ's afflictions"*:

*Now I rejoice in what was suffered for you, and I fill up in my flesh **what is still lacking in regard to Christ's afflictions**, for the sake of his body, which is the church. (Colossians 1:24; emphasis added)*

Chapter Six

GOD'S SOLUTION TO HIS DILEMMA: PART II

The second part of God's solution to His dilemma is founded in the fact that no matter how great the loving ability or capacity of an individual, he or she cannot fully love without intimate *knowledge* of the object of that love. In other words, to love God, we must *know* God; we must have an intimate knowledge *of* God. To achieve our creation purpose of entering eternal life in the loving Fellowship of the Trinity we must *know* the Members of the Fellowship:

> *Now this is eternal life: that they may **know** you, the only true God, and Jesus Christ, whom you have sent. (John 17:3; emphasis added)*

God's conundrum is clear: how could we, the *created*, be brought to a deep heart knowledge of *"the depth of the riches of the wisdom and knowledge of God"*?

> *Oh, the depth of the riches of the wisdom and knowledge of God! How **unsearchable** his judgments, and his paths beyond tracing out! (Romans 11:33; emphasis added)*

In this regard, God has clearly demonstrated His desire to be known by us. The required knowledge of God is encompassed in the knowledge of His knowable attributes. AW Tozer, in <u>The</u>

Knowledge of the Holy, admonishes us that our relationship with God can never exceed our knowledge and appreciation of His attributes. So, the final requirement of the individuals that would be found capable of joining the eternal Fellowship of God is that they experience that which is necessary to enable and obtain a profound, deep, detailed, and intimate knowledge of the attributes of God.

We are best introduced to this discussion by consideration of a dilemma of our own, the palpable presence of our sinful nature. It is in the acknowledgment and exploration of the dark corridors of our innately sinful nature that we see our most desperate need for a new perspective.

> *For what the law was powerless to do in that it was weakened by the sinful nature, God did by sending his own Son in the likeness of sinful man to be a sin offering. And so he condemned sin in sinful man, in order that the righteous requirements of the law might be fully met in us, who do not live according to the sinful nature but according to the Spirit. (Romans 8:3-4)*

Since one of the foundational pillars of Christianity is the humble acceptance of personal responsibility for our sins, most of us would readily claim credit for coming up with this sinful nature of ours completely on our own.

The Bible would suggest otherwise. Quite in contrast to our feigned humility in this regard, the Bible would assure us that every morsel and millisecond of that which exists *outside* of the Uncreated God—including our sinful nature—is indeed part of the creation and therefore created by our Creator God. In other words, we are exactly what God made us. Contrary to popular belief, we did not come up with our sinful nature on our own; *God* gave it to us.

> *For God has bound all men over to disobedience* ***so that*** *he may have mercy on them all. (Romans 11:32; emphasis added)*

As we have discussed, we know that God is perfectly, infinitely efficient in everything that He does. Since our sinful nature is a part of the creation, God must have had a reason for including it. We cannot help but wonder why our Creator God gave us a sinful nature.

> *Why, O LORD, do you make us wander from your ways and harden our hearts so we do not revere you? Return for the sake of your servants, the tribes that are your inheritance. (Isaiah 63:17)*

Not only must there be a reason, but we can be assured that it is a good reason. Further, we can rest assured that the creation would not have been complete—infinitely perfectly complete—in delivering that for which it was brought into being without the inclusion of our sinful nature!

Why would God instill in each of us such a devastating handicap? In giving us a sinful nature, was our loving God really setting us up to fail? After all, He admonished Adam and Eve in the Garden of Eden that they would *"surely die,"* not *"if"* they ate from *"the tree of the knowledge of good and evil,"* but *"when"* they ate of it (Genesis 2:17).

Further exemplifying our concern in this regard is the obvious presence of a persistent pattern of instilled willful disobedience revealed in the history of Israel as recorded by the authors of the Old Testament. As a direct result of the Israelites repeated willful sin, God subjects them to the harsh rule of their oppressive neighbors. The only amelioration of this predicament that is offered to the people of Israel is to "cry out" to the Lord.

This can't help but make us feel a bit uneasy. After all, every one of us cringes at the movies when the story plot includes a teenage boy asking one of his friends to bully a pretty girl just so he can be the hero and rescue the girl he wishes to impress. Are the God-ordained disaster scenarios in our life any different?

This repetitive Old Testament pattern—and its clear extension to our life—can't help but engender difficult questions. Do we really serve a petulant, self-serving God who puts us in difficult scenarios just to get us to cry out for His rescue?

We know the answer to this question. We know that we do not. We know instead that our loving, faithful, compassionate, and merciful God must have a reason for putting us through these circumstances. First of all, we know the only possible motivation behind that reason is His love for us. Further, we know that God is perfectly logical in His reasoning. This loving and logical reason is, in fact, the solution to God's dilemma.

The passage above from Romans is critical to understanding how our sinful nature relates to God's dilemma. The key words that reveal the plan of God are *"so that."* They tell us exactly why we had to be created with a sinful nature. Without our sinful nature, the incarnation, crucifixion death, and resurrection of Jesus Christ all become unnecessary. But, without these key events, there is no demonstration of God's most wonderful attributes of righteousness, holiness, justice, faithfulness, compassion, power, mercy, and love (to name only a few).

Why was it so critical that God demonstrate these attributes in such a compelling manner? This question leads us directly back to God's dilemma. Our sinful nature is not God's dilemma, as so many teach. Instead, it is part of the *solution* to God's dilemma.

Additionally, since our sinful nature would be classified as clearly "evil" by all objective observers, our conclusion begs an even more difficult question: Does this mean that God created evil? If so, why? The follow up question to that one is even worse. It takes us to a place that most of us simply do not want to go. Our line of logic demands that we address the question of whether God really created some people *for the sole purpose* of succumbing to the righteous consequences of their evil deeds— and burning in the fires of hell forever? Most of us who have felt—and therefore know firsthand—the compassion, mercy, comfort, and lavish love of our Savior, struggle with such a question.

We have already established that this revelation of the attributes of God is essential to imparting to us the knowledge of God that allows us to achieve our creation purpose and join the eternal Fellowship of the Trinity. In this regard, what do the necessity of our sinful nature and the creation of evil tell us about the mechanism that God uses to reveal His attributes? Let's begin in the Garden of Eden where the knowledge of good and evil was first obtained by our progenitors.

Chapter Seven

LIFE IN THE GARDEN OF EDEN WAS NOT SO PERFECT AFTER ALL

When most of us think of the Garden of Eden, we revert to the colorful descriptions provided by our childhood Sunday school education. We were told then—and we had no reason to doubt it—that everything in the Garden of Eden was perfect and that eternal life there was God's original plan for mankind. The implied message was clear. God's original plan was for man to still be living there if not for the first manifestation of our sinful nature that resulted in the fall of man and our expulsion from paradise. In other words, mankind would still be blissfully living the Eden dream if Adam and Eve had not messed everything up.

No doubt things were good in Eden—very good. The book of Genesis makes this very clear. But we have to ask ourselves whether everything was really *perfect* in the Garden of Eden. Was continued life in the Garden of Eden for all eternity really God's plan? Could Adam and Eve have loved God in the Garden of Eden with the depth of love that is required to even join the eternal Fellowship of the Trinity—let alone live in it for eternity? Could Adam and Eve have even had a glimmer of truly sacrificially subservient love? After all, there was no "sacrificial" anything in the Garden of Eden. The word "sacrifice" had not even been invented yet. There was no need for it.

What could Adam and Eve have truly known about God in the Garden of Eden? What could they have known of His attributes? Surely, God's attributes of power, glory, and beauty were at least partially on display to Adam and Eve in the magnificence of the Garden of Eden. But, what could Adam and Eve have known of the rest of God's attributes, such as His righteousness, justice, wrath, holiness, faithfulness, compassion, mercy, and love? Further still, had they *really* experienced the fullness of God's power, glory, and beauty in Eden? After all, can there really exist a full appreciation of beauty when there is no ugly?

How can we call Adam and Eve's knowledge of God and their resulting love of God in the Garden of Eden truly intimate without their experiencing the fullness of His most amazing attributes? Surely God possessed these attributes as Adam and Eve walked among the magnificence of the Garden of Eden. Nonetheless, we can also know with equal certainty that there could be no chance of illuminating these attributes and plumbing them to the true depths of their infinite magnificence.

Why not?

We have hinted at and alluded to the answer to this question without naming it. It is time to name it. There was no *contrast* in Eden. There was no darkness to outline the detail of the bright white attributes of God. We take this for granted in our world because of its inherent overabundance of contrast to the attributes of God. Our world is brimming with the darkness of evil to be contrast against the purity of God's eternal attributes. Against the darkness of this world, the purity and detail of God's attributes are magnificently illuminated and precisely defined.

In other words, the bright white details of God's attributes were *invisible* to Adam and Eve in Eden for a lack of contrast. After all, in Eden there was no unrighteousness, injustice, unfaithfulness, selfishness, cruelty, hatred, or evil to be contrast against the infinitely perfect righteousness, justice, faithfulness, generosity, kindness, love, and goodness of God. There was no ugly to accentuate the beauty of God. There was no vulnerability to supply a metric for His power. There was no inglorious to bring out God's glory.

Life in the Garden of Eden wasn't so perfect after all.

Chapter Eight

THE WHITE ROOM ANALOGY

An illustrative analogy revealing the importance of contrast in illuminating the attributes of God is found in consideration of a perfectly illuminated pure white room filled with bright white furniture. This room is so perfectly and intensely illuminated from an infinite number of light sources that it is absolutely devoid of any darkness or shadows. One would intuitively think that our observation of the contents of this room illuminated by infinite sources of white light would be optimal. With a little thought, however, we recognize the error of our logic.

Instead, quite to the contrary, we would be functionally blind in such a room. Without some degree of darkness—shadows— to supply the necessary *contrast* to their shape and detail, the objects in the room would be completely invisible to us. In our bright white, perfectly illuminated room, we would be utterly blind.

In a similar fashion, God had to introduce darkness— contrast—into His creation to optimize the display and perception of His attributes. He had to supply the contrast in order for us to gain an intimate and eternal knowledge of His attributes—an intimate and eternal knowledge of Him—that is capable of rendering us worthy of our creation purpose. Such an infinite capability can only be supplied by the illuminated and detailed exhibition of God's attributes by the depth of contrast, the fullness of darkness found in evil and rebellious sin.

In other words, to show us who and what He is, God had to show us who and what He is not.

Thus, to solve the dilemma of making His chosen created beings worthy of an eternity of loving fellowship, God knew exactly what He was doing when He went skillfully about His masterful creation craft in the ordering of our lives. The creation—and every moment of our lives in it—is specifically and purposefully designed to impart to the heirs of God's kingdom a *knowledge* of God that would allow us to subserviently and sacrificially love the three Persons of the Trinity—and each other—forever. God states precisely this throughout the Bible. Everything in the creation has a purpose and that purpose is to impart knowledge of the *Uncreated* to those in the creation who are called to be heirs to His eternal kingdom.

> *And we pray this in order that you may live a life worthy of the Lord and may please him in every way: bearing fruit in every good work, **growing in the knowledge of God**, being strengthened with all power according to his glorious might so that you may have great endurance and patience, and joyfully giving thanks to the Father, who has qualified you **to share in the inheritance of the saints in the kingdom of light**. (Colossians 1:10-12; emphasis added)*

To instill the knowledge of God that would make His created beings capable of loving the *Uncreated* and therefore capable of joining with and deeply engaging the *Uncreated* in the eternal Fellowship of the Triune Godhead, God had to instill knowledge of His attributes that went infinitely beyond the superficial. He had to supply a deep heart framework upon which knowledge of

Him of *infinite* depth could be constructed. But, just as our "white room" analogy illuminates, the complexities, detail, depth, and fullness of the bright white, infinitely pure attributes of God are impossible to comprehend without contrasting them against *that which they are not*, that which is their opposite.

"That which they are not, that which is their opposite" is what we call "evil" in our world.

Most of us experience immediate revulsion toward any consideration that our wonderfully good God could have it in Him to create the contrasting manifestations of non-God in our world that we call *evil*. When logically considered, however, the facts clearly tell us that He did exactly that. As discussed previously, we know for a fact that God created *all* that has been created. Anything that was not created is, by definition, "*Uncreated*." *Uncreated*, once again by definition, *is* God. (See Tozer, The Knowledge of the Holy)

The manifestations of non-God that we call *evil* do in fact exist in the creation. Further, there is no evidence that these manifestations of evil existed before the creation. If they had, then they would indeed be *Uncreated*. But, as Tozer so skillfully explains, there can only be one *Uncreated* and that *Uncreated* is God. If they had existed before the creation and were in fact *Uncreated*, then they would be God. They are not *Uncreated* and they are not God. The manifestations of non-God that we call *evil* are created.

Thus, God—the only Creator of *all* that has been created—did indeed create the manifestations in our world that we label *evil*.

> *"See, it is I who created the blacksmith who fans the coals into flame and forges a weapon fit for its work. And it is I who have created the destroyer to work havoc; (Isaiah 54:16)*

Moreover, we know that the focal point of evil that is found in the creation is Satan. He is, in fact, repeatedly referred to as *"the evil one."*

> *We know that we are children of God, and that the whole world is under the control of **the evil one**. (1John 5:19; emphasis added)*

All evil appears to have begun with and is manifest in and empowered by Satan—and the Bible makes it real clear that Satan was indeed *created*.

> *"Son of man, take up a lament concerning the king of Tyre and say to him: 'This is what the Sovereign LORD says: "You were the model of perfection, full of wisdom and perfect in beauty. You were in Eden, the garden of God; every precious stone adorned you: ruby, topaz and emerald, chrysolite, onyx and jasper, sapphire, turquoise and beryl. Your settings and mountings were made of gold; on the day **you were created** they were prepared. You were anointed as a guardian cherub, for so I ordained you. You were on the holy mount of God; you walked among the fiery stones. (Ezekiel 28:12-14; emphasis added)*

We can therefore conclude that the manifestations of non-God that we call *evil*, as well as its initiator, Satan, did not exist prior to the creation. Evil, just like the person in whom it is sustained, is a created—not uncreated—entity. God, the Creator of all that has been created, created them. With perfect reasoning and wisdom, God created evil as a perfect and essential part of His perfect creation. If evil is a part of the creation, it has purpose in the creation and is in fact essential to attaining the perfect product of the creation.

Just as the summation of all of God's attributes comprises the knowledge of God, so also, by definition, is the aggregate of all of their respective dark contrasting opposites the very definition of *evil*. In this regard, *evil* becomes almost a word of *summation* that is comprised of many components, all of which are "non-God." Each one of these contrasting components of the summated *evil* is, in turn, necessary to illuminate—to contrast—its respective attribute of God.

For example, to illuminate His attribute of mercy in all of its depth and detail, God had to create a manifestation of evil that is its opposite. In the world in which we exist, this is manifest by the thoughts, plans, and actions of utterly merciless individuals. Similarly, to illuminate His selfless, subservient sacrificial love, God created the opposing constructs of self-centeredness, arrogance, selfishness, pride, and hatred.

Another example is found in the illumination of God's faithfulness. God creates manifestations of unfaithfulness in the individuals whom He brings into our life. As the Bible repeatedly tells us, God's faithfulness is especially highlighted when the marriage covenant is considered. The unfaithfulness we see so often manifest in the marriage covenant is contrasted against the perfect faithfulness of Jesus in His covenant with the Father to rescue His church on the cross of Calvary. None of this is random. It is all by the detailed plan of the All-wise God—and it is all motivated by God's desire for us to obtain our heart's deepest desire and achieve our creation purpose.

Thus, each one of God's many known attributes is illuminated by its opposite, that which is *non-God* and which therefore provides contrast to define the detail and purity of each of God's attributes. This is why in this world we are exposed to (and ourselves also become) mean, stingy, selfish, self-centered, hating, unfaithful, unjust, unrighteous, unholy, unloving, arrogant, prideful, evil human beings.

It was therefore mandatory that evil exist as a critical and functional component of God's eternally perfect creation.

Chapter Nine

SCRIPTURAL ILLUMINATION
OF THE ATTRIBUTES OF GOD

Thus, to brightly contrast the infinitely perfect detail of His attributes, God created "constructs," or creation manifestations, of their respective opposites. Each of God's many known attributes is treated similarly in respect to this provision of illuminating contrast. Evil, the summation of all of these contrasting opposites, thereby exists in the creation as the polar 180-degree opposite of the nature of God.

Most, if not all, of these created evil constructs are manifest in the thoughts and behavior of the individuals to whom we are exposed during our lifetime. As is readily apparent to any repentant Christian, nonetheless, the thoughts and actions of other individuals are not the only sources of contrasting evil in our lives. These dark, contrasting opposites of the attributes of God are manifest in even greater depth in our very own thoughts and behavior.

Thus, in God's perfectly designed creation, we don't just hear, feel, and observe the many manifestations of evil that highlight the detail of God's attributes; we *become* them. We generate them from the depths of our own heart and we, ourselves, are the source of their manifestation in the world. The depth of the knowledge of God that is thereby obtained by our self-generated contrasting darkness far exceeds that superficial knowledge that would have been obtained by observation alone.

Just as our knowledge of the opposing evil contrast is enhanced by the deep immersion into it that occurs when we generate and become evil ourselves, so also are the reflected details of God's attributes enhanced to a greater degree. By *generating* and *being* the depth of the contrast, we optimize the knowledge of God that is gained. This is God's perfect plan to bring our knowledge of Him to a level that will enable us, His created beings, to imitate the deep heart love with which He loves us. As Paul repeatedly admonishes, however, this is of course no endorsement of—or excuse for—our deep dives into the dark depths of sin.

> *But if our unrighteousness brings out God's righteousness more clearly, what shall we say? That God is unjust in bringing his wrath on us? (I am using a human argument.) Certainly not! If that were so, how could God judge the world?*
>
> *Someone might argue, "If my falsehood enhances God's truthfulness and so increases his glory, why am I still condemned as a sinner?"*
>
> *Why not say—as we are being slanderously reported as saying and as some claim that we say—"Let us do evil that good may result"? Their condemnation is deserved. (Romans 3:5-8)*

Nonetheless, all of us have in fact been given a sinful nature by God's omniscient ordination. By this sinful nature, we cannot help but generate darkness. As a result, all of us—by God's masterful design—come to know His attributes to the depth, degree, and quality that have been determined by God in accordance with the grace He gives each of us.

The text of the Bible is brimming with clarifying explanations and illustrative examples of the methodology by which God provides illuminating detail of His attributes by contrasting them against their dark opposites. To help illustrate, we will begin with one of its most obvious examples. In the book of Romans, Paul specifically names some of God's key attributes and the precise creation craft by which God constructs and ordains their display in the lives of the Biblical saints—and thereby in our lives via the written word of God.

Once again, we begin with this example because of the outright boldness of its explanation. God could not make it any clearer. This particular passage discusses the undeniable demonstrations of God's wrath, power, glory, and mercy that are found in the stark dichotomy that exists between those who will be saved and those who will not.

> *What if God, choosing **to show his wrath** and **make his power known**, bore with great patience the objects of his wrath—prepared for destruction? What if he did this **to make the riches of his glory known to the objects of his mercy**, whom he **prepared** in advance for glory—even us, whom he also called, not only from the Jews but also from the Gentiles? (Romans 9:22-24; emphasis added)*

In the entirety of the Bible, there may not be a better-written reminder of how carefully God chooses His words. We *are* those *"objects of his mercy, prepared in advance for glory"*! This life—every bit of it—is about our being prepared for the *"glory"* of God's eternal kingdom. Even the outright evil human beings who populate our life—the *"objects of his wrath—prepared for destruction"* are born by God *"with great patience"* just so that His eternal saints can be exposed to the antithesis of each of His attributes. In regard to the revelation of God's attributes, it can't be stated any clearer. Only by living amongst their antitheses every day of our life can we come to a full knowledge of the attributes of God (being wrath, power, glory, and mercy in this particular passage).

Chapter Ten

UNDERSTANDING THE POINT OF IT ALL

These illustrative Scriptural passages are obviously critical to constructing a functional, Christ-based theology that empowers us to face the arduous trials of every day life. In other words, to walk with Christ in our daily lives, *we must understand the point of it all.* We must understand why we go through what we go through. We must "get" that this life is all about obtaining a deep heart knowledge of the attributes of God. It truly changes everything if we understand that we go through what we go through for a reason—an eternal reason.

This applies to all aspects of our life, but especially to the unpleasant parts. It surely matters if we understand that we are going through all the discord, pain, anxiety, fear, trials, and suffering of this life for a specific purpose. We, by God's grace, can get through almost anything if we know why it is happening and appreciate the eternal rewards—the knowledge of God—that it will bring. In fact, how awesome those trials become when we have weathered them!

But how equally sad it is when we never comprehend what God is trying to teach us—and even worse when we do understand, but stubbornly choose to suffer for nothing. There is simply nothing more pathetic than suffering through the trials without gaining that which they are intended to impart.

Although God's power, beauty, glory, and love were at least partially known to Adam and Eve in the Garden of Eden, a review of some of the most notable of God's other known attributes starkly demonstrates that the available overall knowledge of God was relatively limited in Eden. As previously mentioned, an entire book could be written about the knowledge of God's attributes that came to mankind only as a direct result of the fall of man. The Bible addresses almost every one of God's primary known attributes with specific reference to the ability of the fallen creation to "show" these attributes to us.

Besides the previously mentioned wrath, power, glory, and mercy, another great example is found regarding one of the most scripturally illuminated of God's attributes, His *justice*. Specific references to the display of His justice are found in many places, perhaps the most notable again being found in the book of Romans:

> *But now a righteousness from God, apart from law, has been made known, to which the Law and the Prophets testify. This righteousness from God comes through faith in Jesus Christ to all who believe. There is no difference, for all have sinned and fall short of the glory of God, and are justified freely by his grace through the redemption that came by Christ Jesus. God presented him as a sacrifice of atonement, through faith in his blood.* **He did this to demonstrate his justice**, *because in his forbearance he had left the sins committed beforehand unpunished—he did it* **to demonstrate his justice** *at the present time, so as to be just and the one who justifies those who have faith in Jesus. (Romans 3:21-26; emphasis added)*

How could Adam and Eve have known God's justice in Eden when no injustice existed? Injustice is precisely the contrast against which the brilliant and magnificent details of God's justice can be precisely defined and optimally illuminated. In fact, until Satan brought about the fall of mankind, we have no scriptural evidence that evil had even revealed itself to Adam and Eve. Until they ate of the fruit, there was no evidence of any revelation of the *"knowledge of good and evil"* (Genesis 2:17).

With no contrast between right and wrong, between good and evil, there is no need for, and therefore can be no demonstration of, God's justice. And yet it would be futile to argue that justice is not, in fact, a primary attribute of God and that—in our life quest of the full knowledge of God—knowledge of it is somehow less essential than the knowledge of any of His other attributes. It is clear that an appropriate depth of knowledge of this vital attribute is only attainable in this life of ours, *outside* of Eden.

Paul emphasizes the importance of his lesson on the display of God's justice by rebuking those who say that the Gospel in any way nullifies the importance of adherence to the law established by God. God's set determination of right and wrong demands strict adherence with the threat of due consequences for disobedience. Paul champions the cause of God's justice, thereby emphasizing the importance of our knowledge of it.

> *Do we, then, nullify the law by this faith? Not at all! Rather, we uphold the law. (Romans 3:31)*

One cannot enter into a discussion about God's attribute of justice without mentioning His *grace*. After all, God's grace— made necessary by His justice and motivated by His love, compassion, and mercy—is on full display only in this fallen life of ours. Surely, just like all of God's attributes, God's grace was present in Eden, for God cannot change. But it could not have been visible to Adam and Eve because, once again, there was no reason for its display in Eden. Its foundation is in God's justice.

God's justice, after all, is that part of His inherent nature that demands consequences for disobedience. His justice made grace not only possible, but also critical to the loving salvation of God's saints while still satisfying the demands of the law. In this respect, surely justice and grace illuminate each other in the atoning sacrifice of Jesus. Only in the grace of the cross of Calvary is justice adequately defined.

> *This is what the LORD says: "Let not the wise man boast of his wisdom or the strong man boast of his strength or the rich man boast of his riches, but let him who boasts boast about this: that he **understands** and **knows** me, that I am the LORD, who exercises **kindness**, **justice** and **righteousness** on earth, for in these I delight," declares the LORD. (Jeremiah 9:23-24; emphasis added)*

Chapter Eleven

THE IMPORTANCE OF "NEED"

God's justice and grace are great illustrations of His use of contrast to display His attributes in the creation. They are, nonetheless, only the beginning. In fact, it is readily apparent to even the casual reader that nearly every page of the Bible is laser-focused on the full revelation of the attributes that make up the knowable nature of God.

An expansive discussion of the attributes of God is not the focus of this book. Such a discussion is available from any number of legendary Christian authors, including A.W. Tozer—most notably and concisely in what is considered by most to be his best work, The Knowledge of the Holy.

As is apparent from the attributes already cited, this discussion of God's knowable attributes is instead focused primarily upon those attributes that most obviously serve to illustrate God's use of contrast in the creation to elucidate the detail and purity of the knowledge of God thereby obtained. In the revelation of God's attributes, special emphasis must be placed upon the mediation of "need" by the evil contrast in our lives. A great example of the importance of *need* is found in the revelation of God's kindness.

Yet he has not left himself without testimony: **He has shown kindness** *by giving you rain from heaven and crops in their seasons; he provides you with*

plenty of food and fills your hearts with joy." (Acts
14:17; emphasis added)

Once again, we have to ask ourselves whether God's
kindness could even be recognized in a place like Eden where
such manifestations of contrasting evil as those mentioned in
this passage—drought and famine—never even existed? Surely
God's expansive provision in Eden was a demonstration of His
kindness, but how could Adam and Eve recognize it as such and
appreciate its fullness, having never experienced a lack of it. It
is hard to appreciate the expansive fullness of the food and drink
available in Eden when one has never experienced starvation or
parching thirst. Surely, never better are the innate details of
God's kindness displayed than when it is contrast against the
foil of *need*—and there was no need in Eden.

Similarly, although God's power was on display in the sheer
magnificence of Eden, its detail is further revealed, once again
by *need*, in the post-fall world. The demonstration of God's
power is deserving of special emphasis simply out of respect for
the sheer number of times it is mentioned in the Bible. One
particularly revealing example is again found in the book of
Romans:

> *Yet he did not waver through unbelief regarding
> the promise of God, but was strengthened in his faith
> and gave glory to God, being fully persuaded **that
> God had power** to do what he had promised. This is
> why "it was credited to him as righteousness."*
> *(Romans 4:20-22; emphasis added)*

The book of Romans continues with an explanation that
further amplifies the vital necessity of God's use of contrast.
Paul specifically echoes God's stated reason for acting the way

He did in supporting the rise of Pharaoh over Israel. It was for the specific purpose of *displaying* His power to us. The wording is so clear that even the most stubborn of us cannot deny the revelation of this purpose. Once again, *need* is critical in the display of God's power. Pharaoh was raised up by God to oppress the nation of Israel. In God's masterful plan, Pharaoh became the dark mediator of need. Such need was simply not present in Eden. The need in Egypt resulting from Pharaoh's oppression was perfect to supply the necessary venue for the dramatic and climactic demonstration of the awesome power of God. No one would argue that in the utter destruction of Pharaoh's mighty charioteers, God is convincingly shown to be utterly sovereign over His creation.

> For the Scripture says to Pharaoh: "I raised you up for this very purpose, that I might **display my power** in you and that my name might be proclaimed in all the earth." Therefore God has mercy on whom he wants to have mercy, and he hardens whom he wants to harden.
> One of you will say to me: "Then why does God still blame us? For who resists his will?"
> But who are you, O man, to talk back to God? "Shall what is formed say to him who formed it, 'Why did you make me like this?'" Does not the potter have the right to make out of the same lump of clay some pottery for noble purposes and some for common use? What if God, choosing **to show his wrath** and **make his power known**, bore with great patience the objects of his wrath—prepared for destruction? *(Romans 9:17-22; emphasis added)*

The demonstration of God's attribute of omnipotence goes right to the core of the issue of our salvation. Its importance in our salvation emphasizes that this discussion of the method God uses to teach us about Himself is not just an "extra credit" theological discussion. Perhaps this is best explained in Isaiah chapter 43. God emphasizes that this life is *all* about coming to *know* God. And, most importantly, this knowledge of God is centered in *belief.* That which we are asked to believe is that the God of Abraham, Isaac, and Jacob is indeed God, and that there is no other. We must believe that He is the only God and that the provision of the cross of His Son Jesus is the only salvation.

> *"You are my witnesses," declares the LORD, "and my servant whom I have chosen, so that you may* **know** *and* **believe** *me and* **understand** *that I am he. Before me no god was formed, nor will there be one after me. I, even I, am the LORD, and apart from me there is no savior. I have revealed and saved and proclaimed—I, and not some foreign god among you.*
> *You are my witnesses," declares the LORD, "that I am God. Yes, and from ancient days I am he. No one can deliver out of my hand. When I act, who can reverse it?" (Isaiah 43:10-13; emphasis added)*

To further illustrate the lack of limitations upon His power, God points to some of its most extraordinary demonstrations in the creation, such as the numbering and naming of each of 70 trillion, trillion, trillion stars.

> *He determines the number of the stars and calls them each by name. Great is our Lord and mighty in* **power***; his understanding has no limit. (Psalm 147:4-5; emphasis added)*

This staggering display of power is decisively contrast against the utter void of power found in the false "gods" of this world. Once again, God is showing us who He is by showing us who He is not. At every point, God is quick to point out the contrast between His attributes and those of these false gods. To our knowledge, these false gods did not make their presence known in Eden before the fall. How could God's power be appropriately framed and illuminated without God's demonstration of the relative impotence of these so-called "gods." Repeatedly God's prophets reveal that these idols are the contrast necessary for full revelation of the power of God.

> *"To whom will you **compare** me or count me equal? To whom will you **liken** me that we may be **compared**?*
>
> *Some pour out gold from their bags and weigh out silver on the scales; they hire a goldsmith to make it into a god, and they bow down and worship it.*
>
> *They lift it to their shoulders and carry it; they set it up in its place, and there it stands. From that spot it cannot move.*
>
> *Though one cries out to it, it does not answer; **it cannot save him from his troubles**. (Isaiah 46:5-7; emphasis added)*

It almost seems as if God cannot emphasize enough the display of His power in nearly every story in the Bible. Nonetheless, we cannot forget that the pinnacle of the display of His power is in the Person of Jesus Christ. We cannot help but acknowledge the power that Jesus, the only Son of God, vacated in His incarnation and death. The Biblical emphasis upon God's power may indeed reflect the fact that it was the single attribute most "veiled" in the incarnation of Jesus Christ.

> *God came from Teman, the Holy One from Mount Paran. Selah His glory covered the heavens and his praise filled the earth.*
> *His splendor was like the sunrise; rays flashed from his hand, where **his power was hidden**. (Habakkuk 3:3-4; emphasis added)*

And yet, we simultaneously realize that in these same events in which God's power is most veiled lies the ultimate demonstration of His power. We need go no further than in our knowledge of Jesus, who is the perfection of the power of God. God's power may have been the only attribute veiled in the incarnation of Jesus, and yet it is still that which the incarnation displays best.

> *Jews demand miraculous signs and Greeks look for wisdom, but we preach Christ crucified: a stumbling block to Jews and foolishness to Gentiles, but to those whom God has called, both Jews and Greeks, Christ the **power** of God and the **wisdom** of God. (1Corinthians 1:22-24; emphasis added)*

Surely we find the pinnacle of power in Jesus because we also find the pinnacle of our need met in His redemptive work. *Need*, of any kind, simply did not exist in Eden. Nor did the astonishing knowledge of God that is revealed only in the extremes of our need.

Chapter Twelve

THE EXTREMES IN THE CREATION SHOW US THE EXTREMES IN THE FAITHFULNESS OF GOD

Truly God goes to extraordinary lengths to show us His attributes in the fullness of their glory. His *faithfulness* is no exception. In fact, many would argue that God did some of His best work in the revelation of His attributes when He provided the dark contrast by which His faithfulness is put on full display. Perhaps no attribute mandated as many major modifications to the creation than the introduction of the source of the primary contrast to God's faithfulness: the institution of marriage.

Marriage introduced the venue for the most intensely personal relationships on the face of the earth, being rivaled only by those relationships that result from marriage (namely parent/child and sibling relationships). The foundation of the institution of marriage is the sacred covenant into which two consenting adults commit to truly unique faithfulness. Together, they commit that their relationship will be above all other relationships in regard to intimacy. They commit that they will not venture outside of marriage for that deep, intense, and vulnerable intimacy that should exist only within the marriage covenant. Their commitment is to God. They commit to Him that in regard to the intimacy of matrimony their commitment to their respective spouse is exclusive to all others. They commit to being utterly faithful to God by being utterly faithful to their spouse.

In one of the most amazing of all scriptural passages, Paul tells us that our commitment in marriage mirrors that which Jesus entered into with the Father in regard to His bride, the church.

> *Wives, submit to your husbands as to the Lord. For the husband is the head of the wife as Christ is the head of the church, his body, of which he is the Savior. Now as the church submits to Christ, so also wives should submit to their husbands in everything.*
>
> *Husbands, love your wives, just as Christ loved the church and gave himself up for her to make her holy, cleansing her by the washing with water through the word, and to present her to himself as a radiant church, without stain or wrinkle or any other blemish, but holy and blameless. In this same way, husbands ought to love their wives as their own bodies. He who loves his wife loves himself. After all, no one ever hated his own body, but he feeds and cares for it, just as Christ does the church—for we are members of his body. "For this reason a man will leave his father and mother and be united to his wife, and the two will become one flesh." This is a profound mystery—but **I am talking about Christ and the church**. (Ephesians 5:22-32; emphasis added)*

Perhaps nothing in his or her life impacts the average person more profoundly than their most intense relationship—that found in the marriage covenant. The pure, infinite, and perfect faithfulness of God—one of His most endearing attributes—could not be better illuminated in contrast to the unfaithfulness of mankind repeatedly manifest in the setting of the institution of marriage.

By our full immersion into the covenant of marriage, therefore, God established the perfect foil by which His faithfulness could be maximally illuminated. This immersion means that almost every one of us will witness, experience, or produce in ourselves, unfaithfulness to the institution of marriage. Surely, in one way or another, unfaithfulness to the marriage covenant has impacted nearly every one of us. Either personally, or with friends and family, all of us have been there. Many of us have experienced first hand what it is like to be the actual instigator of unfaithfulness to this most sacred of covenants.

Against this deeply personal and profoundly punishing unfaithfulness of ours is contrast the utterly perfect faithfulness of Jesus to His bride. Jesus, in recognition of the covenant He entered into *with His Father*—just like we enter into our marriage covenant with the Father—stayed upon the cross of Calvary to complete His redemption work. He was faithful to complete the work necessary to save His beloved. Jesus was faithful to the infinite extreme.

> *But now, this is what the LORD says—he who created you, O Jacob, he who formed you, O Israel:*
> *"Fear not, for I have redeemed you; I have summoned you by name; you are mine.*
> *When you pass through the waters, I will be with you; and when you pass through the rivers, they will not sweep over you.*
> *When you walk through the fire, you will not be burned; the flames will not set you ablaze.*
> *For I am the LORD, your God, the Holy One of Israel, your Savior; (Isaiah 43:1-3a)*

Another attribute of God that simply had no chance of ever being displayed without the extremes in dark contrast brought about by the fall of man—and therefore had no chance of being revealed in Eden—is *meekness*. Without the incarnation, ministry, death, and resurrection of Jesus Christ—all necessitated by our sinful human nature—how could we have ever known of this, the crown jewel of subservient, sacrificial love? How would we ever have witnessed that pinnacle display of meekness upon which a foundational knowledge of this most treasured of God's attributes must be based? How would ultimate power, veiled in subservient, sacrificial humility and motivated by nothing short of infinite love, ever have been made known to us? How could our love of God ever have been made perfectly complete without this knowledge of this most endearing of His many attributes? How could we have known of the Biblical emphasis—and therefore the importance—that God obviously places on this attribute of His? How could we have known how to adopt and display this attribute in our own lives without the perfectly modeled display of perfect meekness—infinite power veiled in equally infinite humility—by God Incarnate, Jesus Christ?

> *But God chose the foolish things of the world to shame the wise; God chose the weak things of the world to shame the strong. He chose the lowly things of this world and the despised things—and the things that are not—to nullify the things that are, so that no one may boast before him. (1Corinthians 1:27-29)*

Indeed, many have written entire books describing the historical documentation of God's attributes that can be found on the pages of the Bible. But nowhere else are so many of

God's attributes displayed more brilliantly than in the single event that sits at the pinnacle of the creation: the death and resurrection of Jesus, the incarnate Son of God. In that event, the foundation of the Gospel of Jesus Christ, surely *all* of God's known attributes were on glorious display.

> *I am not ashamed of the gospel, because it is the **power** of God for the salvation of everyone who believes: first for the Jew, then for the Gentile. For in the gospel a **righteousness** from God is **revealed**, a righteousness that is by faith from first to last, just as it is written: "The righteous will live by faith."*
>
> *The **wrath** of God is being **revealed** from heaven against all the **godlessness** and **wickedness** of men who suppress the truth by their wickedness, since **what may be known about God** is plain to them, because God has made it plain to them. For since the creation of the world God's invisible qualities— **his eternal power and divine nature**—have been **clearly seen**, being **understood** from what has been made, so that men are without excuse. (Romans 1:16-20; emphasis added)*

The crucifixion and resurrection of Jesus Christ is central to the revelation of God's power, righteousness, wrath, holiness, sovereignty, wisdom, justice, mercy, omniscience, compassion, grace, and—in the most spectacular of fashion—God's subservient, sacrificial love on display in the meekness of Jesus Christ.

> *But God demonstrates his own love for us in this: While we were still sinners, Christ died for us. (Romans 5:8)*

We build our sanctification knowledge of God upon this most important foundational demonstration of God's attributes. The laying of this foundation is not just the pinnacle moment of the creation, but so also of our individual preparation for the eternity of fellowship that is our creation purpose.

> *Praise the LORD.*
> *I will extol the LORD with all my heart in the council of the upright and in the assembly.*
> *Great are the works of the LORD; they are pondered by all who delight in them.* **Glorious** *and* **majestic** *are his deeds, and his* **righteousness** *endures forever. He has caused his wonders to be remembered; the LORD is* **gracious** *and* **compassionate**. *He provides food for those who fear him; he remembers his covenant forever.* **He has shown his people the power of his works**, *giving them the lands of other nations. The works of his hands are* **faithful** *and* **just**; *all his precepts are* **trustworthy**. *They are* **steadfast** *for ever and ever, done in* **faithfulness** *and* **uprightness**. *He provided redemption for his people; he ordained his covenant forever—**holy** and **awesome** is his name.*
> *The fear of the LORD is the beginning of wisdom; all who follow his precepts have good understanding. To him belongs eternal* **praise**. *(Psalm 111:1-10; emphasis added)*

Chapter Thirteen

THANK GOODNESS THEY ATE THE FORBIDDEN FRUIT!

How could continued life in the Garden of Eden have given Adam and Eve—or their offspring—any hope of gaining the critical knowledge of the foundational attributes of God? Truly, "the fall" changed everything. Without the contrasting display of evil palpably extended to the very heart of man, these Divine attributes, though eternally present and vital to the knowledge of God, would have remained undetected by God's created beings.

Continued life in Eden was never the plan.

Instead, the fall of mankind, our God-ordained sinful nature, and the unspeakable evil that spawns in the dark wastelands of our heart were always part of God's plan. Without them, nothing works. Without them and the necessitated incarnation, crucifixion, and resurrection of Jesus Christ, we have no way to obtain the deep heart knowledge of God that is so vital to our eternal role in the Fellowship to which we have been called. If this wasn't God's chosen plan from the very beginning, the Bible would not tell us that Jesus *"was chosen **before** the creation of the world"* (1Peter 1:20; emphasis added). Our sinful nature and all of the unspeakable evil that resulted from it have always been a most critical and essential part of God's plan.

As we have discussed, our plight in regard to obtaining the necessary knowledge of God is obviously even worse than all this. Even a full written revelation of God's attributes, such as that described in the text of the Bible, is not enough to ensure adequate depth to our knowledge of God. The eternal Fellowship of the Triune Godhead is not business as usual. This is a truly unfathomable relationship to which we have been invited! It is unimaginable in even our wildest dreams. The love exceeds anything to which we have been exposed. It is incomprehensible. No one would deny that the written description of the attributes of God found on the pages of Holy Scripture is critical to obtaining our needed knowledge base. Nonetheless, to say that a written description of the attributes of God is inadequate as a sole source of the knowledge of God is a colossal understatement.

For us—the princes and princesses of the eternal kingdom of God—to gain the depth of knowledge necessary to join the eternal Fellowship of the Uncreated Trinity, we must possess an outrageously deep, a truly scandalous knowledge of the attributes of God—and especially of the subservient, sacrificial love of God. This depth of knowledge can only be enabled by a knowledge of evil—a knowledge of the attribute-illuminating "contrast"—whose intensity rivals the depth of the knowledge of the three Persons of the Trinity that is critically necessary to love them (and each other) in a manner worthy of this most extraordinary Fellowship.

In other words, God knew that He had to take us an incredible step further than just reading about, observing, or even living in the midst of evil; we had to actually *become* the darkness. We couldn't just read about it or watch it from the sidelines. We couldn't just learn this lesson from a classroom lecture. Instead, we had to *become* that lesson. We had to live it. We had to become darkness, embody evil, and generate sin from the unfathomable depths of our hearts. Only then could we actually become the objects of the rescue made possible by the merciful compassion and love exploding from the crucifixion death and resurrection of Jesus Christ. We had to be the object upon which God would display the utter magnificence of His infinitely deep, infinitely subservient, infinitely sacrificial love.

Both of the previously discussed requirements—a demonstration of *how* to love and a deep knowledge of God—mandated the fall of mankind and our rescue by the infinitely perfect subservient, sacrificial love demonstrated by God. Both required that our Creator ordain us with nothing less than a rebellious and sinful nature. Both required the introduction of evil into the creation.

So, despite what many of us have been taught, surely there was nothing good about the state of man in Eden. Adam and Eve neither knew God, nor did they know *how* to truly love Him. Their creation purpose and deepest heart desires were thereby completely beyond their grasp. The preordained fall was critical: rescue from an utterly hopeless eternity by the Object of their creation purpose and deepest heart desire became possible only because mankind fell.

To carry this off, God had to create individuals who were *capable* of filling that vital purpose, and then through the mastery of the creation itself, lead them through the crucible that would turn them into those precise beings with which He could share an eternity of loving fellowship. No matter how notoriously bad the world around us may look, we can be assured that in regard to God's eternal purpose of preparing us for an eternity of loving fellowship with Him, it really is perfect. When we step into eternity after the creation has done its God-ordained and perfect work, we *will* know *how* to love and we will *know* God.

This is the covenant I will make with the house of Israel after that time, declares the Lord. I will put *my laws **in their minds** and write them on their hearts. I will be their God, and they will be my people. No longer will a man teach his neighbor, or a man his brother, saying, 'Know the Lord,' because they will all **know** me, from the least of them to the greatest. (Hebrews 8:10-11; emphasis added)*

And, only by this knowledge will we be enabled to truly love Him in a manner that is worthy of the Fellowship of the Uncreated God.

Chapter Fourteen

"So What?"

Our first reaction to the logic stream revealed in this discussion may be dismissive. In fact, the first words that come to mind might well be a recalcitrant "So what?" We well might ask why this discussion is not just another in a lengthy stream of equally long-winded discourse relegated to the hallways of the seminaries of the world? How is any of this relevant to the "real world" struggles that fill every day of our life? Of what possible importance are the details of the mechanism by which God uses evil to reveal His attributes to us?

Part of the answer to these questions is once again found in our knowledge of the perfection of the Creator—and therefore the perfection of the creation. Knowledge of His perfection provides an obvious and important response. This perfection means that everything we see around us will in fact be proven perfect by the perfection of its ultimate product—us. This is mandated by the fact that we are the perfect creation of a Sovereign Creator who is perfect in everything He does. It logically follows that the purpose of *everything* that happens to us is the perfect achievement of that goal, that product.

In light of our universal recognition of the compassion, mercy, and love of God, the identification of the mechanism by which God obtains His perfection may seem counterintuitive. After all, would a God who *"is love"* really use extreme evil to develop dangerous, troublesome, or challenging scenarios for us, only to have our rescue be solely dependent upon our mandatory response to call upon *Him*—especially since He is in fact the very Individual who created the vexing scenario in the first place?

> *The cords of death entangled me, the anguish of the grave came upon me; I was overcome by trouble and sorrow. Then I called on the name of the LORD: "O LORD, save me!" The LORD is gracious and righteous; our God is full of compassion.* (Psalm 116:3-5)

In this regard, we need to briefly revisit a previous discussion. In our typically human and misguided line of logic, our first reaction is that a scriptural passage like the one above paints *"the LORD"* in a scheming and self-serving light. These are not descriptors that are applicable to the God of Abraham, Isaac, and Jacob. In fact, these attributes are precisely the exact opposite of our infinitely truthful, holy, righteous, and meek God who so perfectly models deeply palpable subservient, sacrificial love. We know that He didn't create us to love and serve Him, as the self-centered needs of some tyrant might demand.

Instead, we know the opposite to be true. God created us out of a desire—not a need—and that desire is to love and serve us—not to be loved and served by us! His desire to share the beauty, adventure, spectacle, glory, and rapturous love of His infinitely marvelous Fellowship was the motivation that drove our creation. We can therefore safely assume that there must be another interpretation of the Divine motivation that drives these troubling events in our life.

If we assume that God's sovereignty and perfection demand that indeed everything we experience has a *purpose* that is in line with God's perfect eternal plan, then the topic of our discussion becomes that purpose. We know that the purpose is not self-serving in regard to our Creator and, therefore, these horrible scenarios that repeatedly play themselves out in our lives must have a purpose in accord with the purpose God had in mind for our creation.

My point is obvious: the only logical conclusion regarding these difficult scenarios placed into our life by a loving and sovereign God is that they are placed there as *lessons*. This life is about obtaining knowledge of the attributes of God. In this regard, these difficult episodes in our life are here to teach us something. If we are put through a series of scripted scenarios in which God controls all of the variables and outcomes, then the only answer that is reasonable—especially within the context of gaining a functional knowledge of God's attributes— is that we are in school. In each case, there is something we must learn and each of these scripted scenarios is a lesson.

If these tough situations are lessons, then this discussion takes on great significance not only in its demonstration of their importance, but also in focusing our attention upon *learning* from the challenges that God has carefully, perfectly, and with infinite omniscience, crafted to minute detail and placed into our life. Our life is all about obtaining a deep heart knowledge of God, a weighty and insightful knowledge of His attributes that will accompany us into an eternity in deep fellowship with Him—and this is the mechanism that God has chosen to teach us this knowledge.

There is therefore only one logical response: we are to learn all we can learn from every one of these lessons.

We must, therefore, accept the fact that we are to actively engage our sanctification process. We have a critical part to play in it. We must remain focused on the task at hand. *We are here to learn about God.* We are here to gain knowledge of the eternal focus of our love. This is serious business. This is our eternity.

If these difficult times are lessons and we are to learn from them, then what precisely are they present in our life to teach us? Surely we are the most pathetic creatures in God's creation if we suffer through these ordeals, all the while ignoring the entirety of their purpose for being in our life in the first place. We have touched upon this before, but further emphasis in this discussion is warranted. To suffer through these lessons without obtaining that knowledge which God wishes to impart to us means that we suffer the deep misery—which this life regularly serves up—all for nothing. In eternity, surely it will become obvious that those instances in which we stubbornly chose to suffer for nothing comprised the most lamentable portions of our life.

> *The bellows blow fiercely to burn away the lead with fire, but the refining goes on in vain; the wicked are not purged out. (Jeremiah 6:29)*

Let Job be our standard-bearer in our quest for the knowledge of God in the midst of suffering. He is a hero of our faith because he bore the most overwhelming suffering, standing fast in his faith in the goodness of God, and was rewarded with a more complete knowledge of God.

> *Then Job replied to the LORD: "I know that you can do all things; no **plan of yours** can be thwarted.*
> *[You asked,] 'Who is this that obscures my counsel **without knowledge**?' Surely I spoke of things I did not **understand**, things too wonderful for me to **know**.*

*["You said,] 'Listen now, and I will speak; I will question you, and you shall answer me.' My ears had heard of you but now my eyes **have seen you**. Therefore I despise myself and repent in dust and ashes." (Job 42:1-6; emphasis added)*

So, instead of railing against God (or worse, against those individuals that He has placed in our life as mediators of our misery) for the suffering we must endure, all logic demands that we take a completely different "eternal" perspective toward these difficult scenarios that seem to serially and uniformly populate every human life.

Instead of anger, we should respond with wonder.

We should respond with amazement at the magnificence of our Teacher and the tools that He uses to teach us these eternal lessons. Even in the most difficult of situations, this amazement cannot help but lead to praise, thanksgiving, and joy.

Be joyful always; pray continually; give thanks in all circumstances, for this is God's will for you in Christ Jesus. (1Thessalonians 5:16-18)

Further, this wonder of ours at the magnificence of God's plan will be that which empowers our deep meditation upon the God-ordained lesson that accompanies each of these unique scenarios. We must learn. We must advance in our knowledge of the nature of God and implement this knowledge in an eternity-based perspective with which we will greet each subsequent challenging scenario. We must learn the lessons found in the difficulty that God orchestrates into our life.

We can logically deduce that these lessons are brought into our life with the specific purpose of turning us more into the likeness of Jesus Christ, specifically in regard to our knowledge of God and our ability to love in a subservient and sacrificial manner. Unless we know the Father as Jesus knows Him, we cannot love Him like Jesus does. Loving the Father like Jesus does is nothing less than the bright white foundation of the Fellowship to which we have been called. Further, unless we learn to love each other as Jesus loves us, we cannot hope to love all who inhabit the eternal Fellowship to which we have been invited. We learn about loving God by loving one another, just as Jesus commanded.

> *"A new command I give you: Love one another.*
> *As I have loved you, so you must love one another."*
> *(John 13:34)*

In each of these life scenarios that we encounter every day of our life, therefore, God places His righteousness, holiness, faithfulness, wisdom, omniscience, sovereignty, justice, power, compassion, beauty, mercy, grace, glory, meekness, and subservient sacrificial love on full display. We can read about these attributes in the Bible. We are even invited to a deep understanding of these attributes by the many illuminating Biblical stories that are used to bring these attributes to life.

Nonetheless, God alone designed us—our bodies, souls and hearts—and knows well that just reading about His attributes, even in the most perfectly composed book ever written, is not enough. He knows we need to *experience* His attributes. We need to know His justice, be rescued by His faithfulness, embrace the glory of His power displayed, delight in the beauty that explodes from His innate Being, seek to meekly submit in our power as Jesus modeled, and then fall into the warmth of the sacrificially loving embrace of our Savior. We must experience God's attributes in real life.

What are the mechanics by which we can best do this? How can we use what God has provided in our life to achieve that for which we are suffering? Most importantly, our accompanying meditation must focus upon each of God's individual attributes. This is precisely why such saints as A.W. Tozer have spent so much time writing about them and pushing us to explore them in the writings of the ancient Christian writers and hymnists. We can, being spirited forward by these inspired writings, not only learn them, but also understand, explore, and experience God's attributes.

None of what we experience in this life makes any sense without this perspective. But, with this perspective in hand, we are thereby enabled to maximize that which is available for us to learn about our amazing God, His Fellowship, and each other. We must cling hard to the knowledge of God. And then we must actually love.

Most importantly, our learning experienced is optimized when we maximally exploit every scenario and fearlessly step out in faith to love God by *loving each other*. It is all a journey. Every relationship matters. Every chance to love matters. Every opportunity to reject fear and step toward God by embracing the love inherent to the Fellowship is a step toward our eternity.

> *The only thing that counts is faith expressing itself through love. (Galatians 5:6b)*

Loving in every situation with every individual must be our goal. Forgiving the unforgivable, loving the unlovable, and running hard after the wellbeing of even our enemies develops in us all the necessary mettle, pluck, and vigor so critical to the eternity God has planned for us. It is our life and it is our eternity. And all are steps toward bringing true meaning to this otherwise seemingly meaningless life of ours.

Understanding God's dilemma and His amazing solution to that dilemma indeed answers almost all of our most difficult questions. We wonder about the presence of evil in God's creation. We see bad things happening to good people and good things happening to bad people. We cannot help but wonder where our God—Who has demonstrated how much He treasures justice—is when we see evil running rampant. Further still, in the honest self-appraisal that can only accompany the indwelling of our hearts by our Savior Jesus, we see the blackness of our own hearts. All is understood only in God's magnificent solution to His dilemma and our resulting acquisition of the knowledge of the Holy God.

Chapter Fifteen

AT WHAT COST?

Surely God went to great detail and truly *infinite* expense to carry out His amazing plan. His presentation of audible, visual, and palpable manifestations of evil to the sons and daughters of eternity in order to perfectly contrast and illuminate His many attributes came at a cost that is unknowable to those of us who are the direct benefactors.

First of all, we can know without doubt that the creation of evil, the creation of all that is non-God, was not a pleasant experience for God. God hates evil and it clearly grieved Him that its creation was necessary.

> *The LORD saw how great man's wickedness on the earth had become, and that every inclination of the thoughts of his heart was only **evil** all the time. The LORD was **grieved** that he had made man on the earth, and **his heart was filled with pain**.*
>
> *So the LORD said, "I will wipe mankind, whom I have created, from the face of the earth—men and animals, and creatures that move along the ground, and birds of the air—**for I am grieved that I have made them**." (Genesis 6:5-7; emphasis added)*

God nonetheless knew that the creation of evil was the only way that His attributes could be known in the depth and detail deserving of the heirs of His kingdom. That depth and detail of His attributes is made readily apparent by the equally intense complexity of their contrasting evil components that are manifest in those around us—and in ourselves.

We show our extreme naiveté when, at first glance, the "expense" to God for His provision of this evil contrast might not seem to be deserving of the descriptor "infinite." After all, He is God. There is no expense that He cannot bear. Since He created every metric that we might apply to measure *expense*, we logically deduce that He can always "just create more." The word "expense" seems meaningless in its application to the Divine Creator God.

Only our acknowledged lack of comprehension of the magnitude of the gap between created and *Uncreated* excuses our naiveté in this regard. That being said, even in our naiveté, all of us would readily agree that in His incarnation, surely Jesus traversed an infinite expanse between the *Uncreated* and the created. Even though scripture tells us that we are made in the image of God, nothing in the creation is—by definition— actually even remotely *like* the *Uncreated*. In this light, surely the word *infinite* accurately describes what the Trinity gave up when Jesus fully accepted—for all eternity—the role of Mediator between God and man, between the created and the *Uncreated*.

> *But when the time had fully come, God sent his Son, born of a woman, born under law, to redeem those under law, that we might receive the full rights of sons. (Galatians 4:4-5)*

Further still, the foundational love of the eternal Fellowship of the Trinity was proven to be *infinitely* subservient and sacrificial in nature by the magnitude of the disruption the

Trinity suffered in the death and resurrection of Jesus Christ. In that event, all three Members of the Trinity suffered infinitely that we might gain eternal life.

Infinite is the only word that can describe the grief of the adoring Son in voluntarily becoming what is most abhorrent to His Father. Equally infinite is the unknowable grief of the Father found in the unleashing of His wrath—mandated by His infinitely perfect justice—upon the Son with Whom He has fellowshipped for eternity in indescribable love. Could the subservient and sacrificial nature of God's love for us be better demonstrated? Surely, no better is God's crowning attribute of love illustrated, illuminated, defined, and glorified than in the crucifixion's selfless and sacrificial atonement for the sins of God's eternal heirs.

> *Your attitude should be the same as that of Christ Jesus: Who, being in very nature God, did not consider equality with God something to be grasped, but made himself nothing, taking the very nature of a servant, being made in human likeness.*
>
> *And being found in appearance as a man, he humbled himself and became obedient to death— even death on a cross! (Philippians 2:5-8)*

Moreover, the infinite cost of our admission to the eternal Fellowship is further manifest in the necessary creation of individuals who would never achieve the creation purpose of joining the eternal Fellowship of the Triune Godhead. After all, God also spent His creation love on those among us who will not accept the free gift of salvation found in the shed blood of Jesus. What great cost to our infinitely loving God to exchange the eternal salvation of the chosen for the eternal damnation of unrepentant non-believers.

*For I am the LORD, your God, the Holy One of Israel, your Savior; I give Egypt for your ransom, Cush and Seba in your stead. Since you are precious and honored in my sight, and because I love you, **I will give men in exchange for you**, and **people in exchange for your life**. (Isaiah 43:3-4; emphasis added)*

They who are not saved have, as their only creation purpose, the illumination of the attributes of God to those who will carry this knowledge of God into the eternal Fellowship of subservient, sacrificial love that is the eternal kingdom of God.

*What if God, choosing to **show** his **wrath** and **make his power known, bore with great patience the objects of his wrath**—prepared for destruction? (Romans 9:22; emphasis added)*

How incalculable is the cost to God in creating beings destined for hell for all eternity—all to display His attributes to those who would spend eternity with Him in fellowship. After all, if there are "chosen"—and the Bible repeatedly emphasizes this fact—then there are also "unchosen."

*But what does the Scripture say? "Get rid of the slave woman and her son, for the slave woman's son will **never** share in the inheritance with the free woman's son." (Galatians 4:30; emphasis added)*

Now to you who believe, this stone is precious. But to those who do not believe,

"The stone the builders rejected has become the capstone,'" and,

"A stone that causes men to stumble and a rock that makes them fall." *They stumble because they disobey the message—which is also **what they were destined for**.*

*But you are a **chosen** people, a royal priesthood, a holy nation, a people belonging to God, that you may declare the praises of him who called you out of darkness into his wonderful light. (1Peter 2:7-9; emphasis added)*

*But these men blaspheme in matters they do not understand. They are like brute beasts, creatures of instinct, born **only** to be caught and **destroyed**, and like beasts they too will perish. (2Peter 2:12; emphasis added)*

That which we must learn from the presence of these individuals who unrepentantly perpetrate evil in the world around us—must be incredibly important to the fulfillment of our creation purpose if, in order to achieve it, God was willing to create human beings destined *"only"* to face such a horrible eternity. The knowledge imparted by their presence is critical to the whole point of the creation. God *had* to teach us about Himself. We must know Him to love Him—and loving Him for eternity, our deepest heart desire, is the foundation of joining the eternal Fellowship of God, our creation purpose—and the purpose of the creation. The existence of these individuals therefore serves God's plan; to show us who He is, God had to show us who He is not. To show us what He is like, God had to show us what He is not like. This is their explicit role.

*Furthermore, since they did not think it worthwhile to retain the **knowledge** of God, he gave them over to a depraved mind, to do what ought not to be done. They have become filled with **every kind of wickedness, evil, greed and depravity**. They are full of envy, murder, strife, deceit and malice. They are gossips, slanderers, God-haters, insolent, arrogant and boastful; they invent ways of doing evil; they disobey their parents; they are senseless, faithless, heartless, ruthless. (Romans 1:28-31; emphasis added)*

This knowledge of God attained through our interacting with these individuals and experiencing the evil they perpetrate is foundational in God's plan for our life that has as its primary motivation God's desire to turn us into individuals who are capable of loving the three Persons of the Trinity (and each other) for eternity. The math is simple. No knowledge of God = no love of God. No love of God = inability to join the Fellowship. The fullness of that which is gained is unknowable to us, the created. Equally so, the proportional expense of that which is sacrificed is also unknowable. And yet we can be assured that God's infinitely all wise, omniscient, omnipotent, and glorious purpose far outweighs even the steep cost of the unsaved.

The facts are clear. We are simply incapable of comprehending *infinite*. Nonetheless, we can rest assured that the word "infinite" was created specifically with its most magnificent purpose being the description of what God paid for our salvation. Only in our first step into eternity will we come to the true knowledge of the definition of that word as it relates to the gift that we have been given. For what do any of us have except that which has been given to us? Just as a pot has no shape, form, or use other than that given it by the potter, so also are we only that which God has made us and can do only that which God has empowered us to do.

> Yet, O LORD, you are our Father. We are the clay, you are the potter; we are all the work of your hand. (Isaiah 64:8)

Chapter Sixteen

IN SUMMARY

The Fellowship of the Triune Godhead is eternal. Just as this Fellowship will never have an end, so also it never had a beginning. It has always been and will always be. It, just like every attribute of God, is infinite. Remarkably, the foundation of this amazing Fellowship is *love*: subservient, sacrificial love. *"God is love."* (1John 4:16)

The natural byproduct of a fellowship that is based upon subservient, sacrificial love must be the desire to *share* the fellowship, the desire to love. It cannot be anything else. It is precisely in this desire to lovingly share their Fellowship that the three Persons of the Trinity *created*. They created individuals with whom to share the Fellowship. They created individuals to love. These individuals are the purpose of all that has been created. *We* are the end product, the goal of God's creation.

Thus, the creation as we know it very literally exploded out of this Fellowship as a predictable, relentless, and in fact inevitable consequence of the nature of the Fellowship. The Members of the Trinity didn't have to think about this. No discussion was needed. The desire to create was as innately natural to God as any of His attributes. The desire to share the Fellowship by creation was one and inseparable with all of the attributes of the three Persons of the Trinity. Their desire to share the Fellowship by creation was so deeply in concert with every one of their attributes—and their joy so great in doing so—that they simply could not help themselves!

And so they created.

Most certainly, they did not create to *be* loved. They did not create for the purpose of fulfilling a need of their own. The three Persons of the Trinity simply acted in concert with their intrinsic nature. This may seem confusing at first since the Bible repeatedly tells us that God's *command* is for us to love Him.

> *"Teacher, which is the greatest commandment in the Law?"*
>
> ***Jesus*** *replied: " **'Love the Lord your God with all your heart and with all your soul and with all your mind.'** This is the first and greatest commandment. And the second is like it: 'Love your neighbor as yourself.' All the Law and the Prophets hang on these two commandments."* *(Matthew 22:36-40; emphasis added)*

Such statements, when isolated apart from the rest of the written word of God, can and have been misinterpreted as describing the self-serving demands of a menacing, self-centered, and needy God. They are in fact the exact opposite.

God does not command us to love Him in response to a need of His. Quite to the contrary, God commands us to love Him because He knows that loving Him is our deep heart desire and the foundation of joining and thriving in the Fellowship of the Trinity. We were created for that Fellowship. In order to gain access to it we had to be created in God's image—and God's deepest heart desire is to love, not to be loved. What a glorious blessing that God loved us so much as to make our heart like His in this regard! He knew that the only way to enable us to join the Fellowship was if our deepest heart desire was to love Him, just like His is to love us.

Thus, when God commands us to love, it is not to fill a void, a need, or a deficiency in Him, but instead because He loves us: He knows that loving Him is the exclusive pathway to fully and resplendently sating the very deepest desire of our heart. In other words, God's command to love Him, instead of being a self-serving demand, is nothing short of a stunning act of love. He wants desperately for our deepest heart desire to be fulfilled in the Fellowship, just like His has been for all eternity.

In fact, it can therefore be logically deduced that God's deep heart desire to love us is fulfilled only when our deepest heart desire is fulfilled in loving Him. Exactly this is the foundational subservient sacrificial love of the eternal Fellowship of the Trinity. In this reciprocating love, the Fellowship is nothing less than a rapidly accelerating feedback loop. Love feeds upon and is sated by love—and then, in utter subservience, immediately reciprocates with even more love. And so the cycle infinitely and eternally accelerates. It is a spontaneously occurring, utterly independent, self-reciprocating circle of love whose very nature fuels an infinitely accelerating and timeless dance between the participants.

And *this* is the eternal dance to which we have been invited.

For surely our creation purpose is to join this Fellowship as royal heirs to the eternal kingdom of God.

> *For he chose us in him before the creation of the world to be holy and blameless in his sight. In love he predestined us to be adopted as his sons through Jesus Christ, in accordance with his pleasure and will—to the praise of his glorious grace, which he has freely given us in the One he loves. (Ephesians 1:4-6)*

To join this Fellowship based upon subservient sacrificial love, obviously one must love. Love, by its very definition, must be directed toward another individual. To love another individual, one must not only know *how* to love them, one must *know* them. The better they are known, the more intimately they can be loved, and the better the participation in the Fellowship.

> *And this is my prayer: that your **love** may abound more and more in **knowledge** and **depth of insight**, (Philippians 1:9)*

To achieve our creation purpose, therefore, we need knowledge of God that is of such incredible depth that it can enable the ensuing fellowship to plumb the deep heart of God. We need to know the three Persons of the Triune Godhead in such depth as to allow a love that is worthy of their infinitely perfect Fellowship. Since that depth is, by definition, also infinite, supplying that knowledge is a daunting task indeed. And yet, critical to the achievement of our creation purpose is our acquisition of exactly this, the fullest possible knowledge of God, the *"fullness of God."*

> *I pray that out of his glorious riches he may strengthen you with power through his Spirit in your inner being, so that Christ may dwell in your hearts through faith. And I pray that you, being rooted and established in love, may have power, together with all the saints, to grasp how wide and long and high and deep is the love of Christ, and to know this love that surpasses knowledge—that you may be **filled** to the measure of all the **fullness of God**. (Ephesians 3:16-19; emphasis added)*

It is in assuring our acquisition of this knowledge that God therefore faced an unfathomable dilemma. The *Uncreated* had to devise a way to impart deep heart knowledge of the attributes of the Persons of the Trinity that could enable the *created* recipients to actually fellowship with the *Uncreated*—a seemingly impossible feat. For what can the created know of the *Uncreated*? All that the created can actually know, after all, is (once again, by definition) *created*.

So, how does one go about enabling created individuals to attain knowledge of a Being—an Uncreated Being—that would thereby allow true love of that Being who is so *utterly unlike them*? How exactly does one tell the finite about the *Infinite*? How does one tell a being with finite attributes about a Being whose every attribute is best described by the literal definition and application of the word "infinite"? More specifically, how does one convey knowledge of a Being who is so utterly unlike anything in the creation in regard to purity, perfection, and infinitude?

An analogy that serves to best illustrate this problem is that of the *infinitely* white room. Although this bright white, perfectly lit room may be full of objects, if it is truly infinitely white, such that no darkness resides there at all, then the objects would be as invisible as if they did not exist at all. If there is no contrast—no darkness—by which the details of the bright white objects can be distinguished, they are in fact rendered invisible.

And so also would the attributes of the Uncreated God be so infinitely and perfectly pure—so unlike mankind—that they would remain, very simply, *invisible*. For example, the infinite faithfulness of God means nothing without the contrast provided by the *unfaithful*. The same is true for all of the attributes of God—His justice, righteousness, mercy, goodness, power, and love—to name just a few. They all need their polar opposites to bring out their infinite detail—and a detailed knowledge of the attributes of God is precisely what is needed to join Him in loving fellowship.

Thus, to deliver knowledge of His infinite attributes, God had to show us their finite opposites. And that is precisely what this life of ours is all about. Further, God did not give us a life limited to just observing and interacting with these evil opposites, like injustice, unfaithfulness, and hatred. The intensity of the Fellowship to which we have been invited mandated that He go one step further.

One giant step.

After all, God's plan is that we will join in truly deep fellowship manifest by the extraordinary depths of subservient, sacrificial love that are the hallmark of the eternal Fellowship of the Trinity! To do this, our knowledge of the attributes of the eternal Creator God had to go beyond that which is obtained by simple observation and superficial interaction.

In other words, God knew that in order to enable a deep heart knowledge that would allow a love worthy of His eternal Fellowship, He would need for those critical contrasting polar opposites of His infinitely pure attributes to be generated from and manifest *in* the very hearts of the created heirs to His kingdom. It was not enough that we just observe or bump into the evil, the unfaithfulness, and the hatred; we had to *be* the source of the darkness. We had to *be* the generating source of the dark contrast against which the fullness of the attributes of God could be brightly illuminated. The true height of eternal fellowship that God desired for His created beings could only result from an opposing, equally profound depth of depravity. Only in this *self*-generated darkness can our hearts experience the depth of contrast against which the perfect detail of every one of God's attributes can be known.

It was precisely in the lack of this illuminating contrast that life in the Garden of Eden was found wanting. Continual life there without the fall of mankind was never God's plan. Adam and Eve may have "messed things up," but it was all part of God's perfectly orchestrated plan!

Surely God's power, glory, and beauty were at least partially on display in the magnificence of Eden. And yet, what could Adam and Eve have known of the rest of God's attributes, such as His justice, righteousness, wrath, holiness, faithfulness, compassion, mercy, and love? Can one really understand justice if there is no injustice? Can one really understand any of these attributes without their contrasting opposites? Further still, had Adam and Eve *really* experienced the fullness of God's power, glory, and beauty in Eden? After all, can there really exist a full appreciation of beauty when there is no ugly? God had to introduce the shadowy, finite darkness to display the pure, infinite light.

And thus God gave a sinful nature to all mankind— especially to every one of the chosen heirs to His eternal kingdom.

We must think this through. We all naturally hold tenaciously to the belief that our thoughts and decisions are 100% our own doing. It is nonetheless also quite clear that the thoughts and decisions that are the hallmark of the life we live are foundationally based upon our genetic makeup combined with the environmental influences in which we live and to which we have been exposed (era, geography, society, family, friends, experiences, relationships—to name but a few). In regard to both of these influences (our genetic makeup and the environmental influences in our life), no one would disagree that they are entirely under God's sovereign discretion. Bottom line: we are 100% that which God has made us.

*For **we are God's workmanship**, created in Christ Jesus to do good works, which God prepared* *in advance for us to do. (Ephesians 2:10; emphasis added)*

*Therefore, my dear friends, as you have always obeyed—not only in my presence, but now much more in my absence—continue to work out your salvation with fear and trembling, **for it is God who works in you to will and to act according to his good purpose.** (Philippians 2:12-13; emphasis added)*

For you created my inmost being; you knit me together in my mother's womb. (Psalms 139:13)

After all, we have nothing that was not given to us by God and are nothing that was not determined by God. We didn't choose the year or location of our birth, our parents, our family, our environment, or our early life environment—to name just a few. Although some might argue that many of our subsequent personal decisions may ultimately have an impact on resulting environmental factors, we can also see that even the choices we make in these decisions are in fact still based upon the prior influence of God.

I know, O LORD, that a man's life is not his own; it is not for man to direct his steps. (Jeremiah 10:23)

With these facts in mind, it is readily apparent that we had nothing to do with placing the manifestations of evil in our hearts. They are embodied in our God-ordained, God-apportioned, God-designed sinful nature. The great philosophers of every age have questioned God's very existence based upon the presence of the unabashed evil that surrounds us.

They asked how a loving God could exist—and still allow such evil.

The Bible's answer to them is straightforward: God not only "allows" all of this evil that fills every part of our life, He *sends* it—all of it. He sends the manifestations of evil into our life with His divine eternal purpose being achieved by nothing less—and all being motivated solely by the loving goodness of His heart. The evil manifest in our surrounding environment during every moment of our life—including that which is generated from the dark recesses of our very own heart—is all part of God's plan to bring His chosen heirs into the Fellowship of the *Uncreated*.

Despite the hardships imposed by our sinful nature, we can be assured of its importance. God's infinite perfection and sovereignty assure us that no matter how confusing, painful, illogical, and fearful the events of our life and the thoughts and actions generated by our sinful nature may seem to be, they are exactly God's plan for us. God's perfection demands that 10,000 years from now, He has precisely the eternity, precisely the Fellowship that He desires. In light of His perfection and sovereignty, it is silly of us to think that God might someday find Himself wringing His hands over the prior lives of the eternal heirs to His kingdom. As we have discussed, the ultimate product of God's creation will be precisely as He has ordained it to be—and it will be perfect.

And best of all, we can also be assured that no matter how disastrous our life may seem, God's orchestration of every event was motivated by His love for us. No matter how painful and fearful these moments may be, we can be assured that God's heart is *for* us. He has planned these moments perfectly for our *eternal* wellbeing. The facts are clear. God has the most amazing eternity planned for each of us, and the very rock bottom foundation of that eternity are the trials, relationships, challenges, pain, and suffering that He alone sends our way in this life.

> *All this is evidence that God's judgment is right, and as a result you will be counted worthy of the kingdom of God, for which you are suffering. (2Thessalonians 1:5)*

Knowing that the love of God is the foundational motivation behind *all* of the events of our life—both good and bad—changes everything. This fact assures us that from every situation we can and must glean knowledge of our Creator. The resulting change in the perspective with which we approach the relational events of our life allows us to respond as if they are all learning opportunities sent by a loving God.

In other words, instead of lashing out at the individuals in our life to whom we attribute evil—we call these people *enemies*—we can resist this worldly response and instead do exactly that which Jesus has asked of us. We can love them. Loving the unlovable is possible only when we acknowledge that the true instigator behind these attacks is a loving God. Only then can we be assured that this is an opportunity for growth in our knowledge of Jesus and thereby respond with *"faith expressing itself in love."* (Galatians 5:6b) Only with this perspective in hand is loving everyone in our life—including and especially our enemies—even remotely possible.

To find assurance that the love of God is behind these relational trials, we have only to look to the most amazing moments of the creation. We have only to recognize God's loving motivation behind His steadfast guarantee of our eternity found in the Gospel of Jesus Christ. The crucifixion and resurrection of Jesus Christ are personal. They are about you and they are about me. God made it that way. He wanted us to rest assured that in any moment of our desperate, anxious life, we have a place to go to know His true heart and to experience His peace, rest, power, and love: the foot of the cross of Christ. There, and only there, does everything in this life of ours make sense.

It is in the crucifixion and resurrection of Jesus Christ—and in the substitution of His obedient righteousness for our sinful rebellion—that we partake of the most magnificent aspect of the creation. We become active participants in God's perfect plan to teach us about Himself. We actually become nothing less than the object of the greatest single act of subservient, sacrificial love in all eternity.

In humbly and subserviently accepting this gift of atonement for our sins, we volitionally and decisively place ourselves *below* our Savior. We place His will, His desires, and His commands above our own. We die to self. In dying to self we also learn to put the desires of all—including not only those of the Trinity, but also those of our fellow saints—above our own. Truly, the circumstances of this moment of our salvation are unique to all of us. Nonetheless, in this moment—and its subsequent fulfillment in our reciprocating love of one another—is found the pinnacle of subservient sacrificial love in *all* of our lives.

It is vital that we understand that it is only "in" Jesus that we can join the Fellowship of the *Uncreated*. We are utterly unequipped otherwise. The role of Jesus as Mediator between the created and the *Uncreated* involves even more than the forgiveness of our sins and the instillation of His righteousness. We must remember where we stand as created beings in relation to the *Uncreated* God. We as created cannot possibly connect in fellowship to the *Uncreated*—the chasm between us is very literally infinite and unbridgeable from our side. The only way for us to enter into the Fellowship of the *Uncreated* is *in* an

Uncreated Member of that Fellowship. Jesus is the One chosen before time to be that Mediator. We must be *in* Him and *remain* in Him—and He *in* us—to join the Fellowship. He is that Mediator who remains simultaneously *in* us *and in* God—and this for all eternity.

> *"My prayer is not for them alone. I pray also for those who will believe in me through their message, that all of them may be one, Father, just as you are in me and I am in you.* **May they also be in us** *so that the world may believe that you have sent me. I have given them the glory that you gave me, that they may be one as we are one:* **I in them and you in me.** *May they be brought to complete unity to let the world know that you sent me and have loved them even as you have loved me.* (John 17:20-23; emphasis added)*

In Jesus we are given the connection to the Fellowship that is encompassed in the word "holy." In this, Jesus is our only hope. As the only eternal Mediator who is both God and man, Jesus is the *only* possible Mediator. Without Jesus Christ, without the very special relationship that is offered by the Gospel of Jesus Christ, we never see the Fellowship. We never achieve our creation purpose or have our deepest heart desire satisfied.

> *What is more, I consider everything a loss compared to the surpassing greatness of knowing Christ Jesus my Lord, for whose sake I have lost all things. I consider them rubbish, that I may gain Christ and be found in him, not having a righteousness of my own that comes from the law, but that which is through faith in Christ—the*

righteousness that comes from God and is by faith. (Philippians 3:8-9)

This is why it is vital that we follow the example of the cross of Christ. In it we learn the "how" of loving. In it is found the perfectly exemplified subservient sacrificial love that is the hallmark of the Fellowship of the Trinity and which we must mimic to *"remain in"* Jesus.

> *"I am the true vine, and my Father is the gardener. He cuts off every branch in me that bears no fruit, while every branch that does bear fruit he prunes so that it will be even more fruitful. You are already clean because of the word I have spoken to you.* **Remain in me, and I will remain in you.** *No branch can bear fruit by itself; it must* **remain in** *the vine. Neither can you bear fruit unless you* **remain in** *me.*
>
> *"I am the vine; you are the branches. If a man* **remains in me and I in him**, *he will bear much fruit; apart from me you can do nothing. If anyone does not remain in me, he is like a branch that is thrown away and withers; such branches are picked up, thrown into the fire and burned. If you* **remain in** *me and* **my words remain in you**, *ask whatever you wish, and it will be given you. This is to my Father's glory, that you bear much fruit, showing yourselves to be my disciples.*
>
> *"As the Father has loved me, so have I loved you. Now* **remain in** *my love.* **If you obey my commands, you will remain in my love**, *just as I have obeyed my Father's commands and* **remain in** *his love. I have told you this so that my joy may be in you and that*

*your joy may be complete. **My command is this: Love each other as I have loved you.** Greater love has no one than this, that he lay down his life for his friends. You are my friends **if you do what I command**. I no longer call you servants, because a servant does not know his master's business. Instead, I have called you friends, for everything that I learned from my Father I have made known to you. You did not choose me, but I chose you and appointed you to go and bear fruit—fruit that will last. Then the Father will give you whatever you ask in my name. **This is my command: Love each other.** (John 15:1-17; emphasis added)*

In this we must become "like" Jesus.

For those God foreknew he also predestined to be conformed to the likeness of his Son, that he might be the firstborn among many brothers. (Romans 8:29)

And we, who with unveiled faces all reflect the Lord's glory, are being transformed into his likeness with ever-increasing glory, which comes from the Lord, who is the Spirit. (2Corinthians 3:18)

*Do not lie to each other, since you have taken off your old self with its practices and have put on the new self, which is being renewed in **knowledge** in **the image of its Creator**. (Colossians 3:9-10; emphasis added)*

And only in becoming like Jesus do we gain the true capability to subserviently and sacrificially love the three Persons of the

Triune Godhead. Without this capability, we cannot experience fellowship with the *Uncreated*.

If subservient, sacrificial love is the foundation of the eternal Fellowship of the three Persons of the Trinity, then it is *everything*. It is unsurpassed in importance when compared to anything else that we shall carry from this life into the next. The capability to love in such a manner is not of a superficial variety, such as that which can be conveyed in even the most complex of didactic lectures. Indeed, a capability of such profound importance can only be learned by observation of—and by participation in—the passion of Christ. To learn it to an infinitely perfect degree—an obligatory step if we are to enjoy an eternity of loving fellowship with the infinite and *Uncreated* God—not only must we observe, but so also become the desperate and hopelessly lost object of that perfectly modeled love…and then reciprocate to God by loving each other in faith.

> *This is how we know what love is: Jesus Christ laid down his life for us. And we ought to lay down our lives for our brothers. (1John 3:16)*

www.ingramcontent.com/pod-product-compliance
Lightning Source LLC
Chambersburg PA
CBHW070544030426
42337CB00016B/2339